The Art & Science of Coaching Series

101

WINNING VOLLEYBALL DRILLS FROM THE AVCA

Edited by Kinda Lenberg

COACHES CHOICE™

ISBN: 1-58518-312-1

Library of Congress Catalog Card Number: 00-105043
Cover Design: Chuck Peters
Cover Photos provided by the AVCA
Diagrams: James Wilkerson
Production Manager: Michelle A. Summers

Coaches Choice
P.O. Box 1828
Monterey, CA 93942
Web Site: http//www.coacheschoiceweb.com

The mission of the American Volleyball Coaches Association is to advance the development of the sport of volleyball by providing coaches with educational programs, a forum for opinion exchange and recognition opportunities. Member participation is vital to the association accomplishing this mission.

The following principles guide the AVCA in the attainment of its goals: To maintain a membership group representative of all levels of competition; to promote the game of volleyball within the general philosophical framework of education; to encourage participation within the highest standards of competition; and to develop greater interest, understanding and support of the sport.

HISTORY OF THE AVCA

In 1981, the AVCA was incorporated as a private non-profit 501-(c)-3 educational corporation. The original Board of Directors consisted of eight NCAA Division I collegiate coaches. A part-time executive director administered the programs.

As the AVCA began to grow and diversify, a full-time executive director was hired in July 1983. An associate director was hired in April 1986 and an administrative assistant in September 1988.

In August 1992, the association moved from San Mateo, Calif., to Colorado Springs, Colo. The staff has increased to the following positions: executive director, director of membership services, director of marketing, director of publications, membership/marketing assistant, membership assistant and part-time bookkeeper. In addition, the association employs interns and other part-time people. In 1986, the Board was increased to 13 members, and in 1987 and 1989, the Board was increased to enfranchise first the high school and then the junior community.

Membership increased steadily from 1981 through 1987 (about 150 new members per year), followed by a 106 percent boom in 1988. Since 1986, high school membership has more than tripled. High school coaches from 46 states and the District of Columbia are members. At the collegiate level, all major NCAA conferences are represented and membership among the club coaches has risen dramatically.

The original members of the AVCA were all intercollegiate coaches who joined together to unite this particular coaching body. They have been the backbone of the association's existence and a united voice determining volleyball's future.

Perhaps the most significant decision was made at the San Francisco convention in 1986, however, when the membership recognized the growing and developing high school and club communities. The name of the association was changed to reflect these growing constituencies. From the original Collegiate Volleyball Coaches Association, the American Volleyball Coaches Association was born with the intent of responding to and serving all volleyball coaches.

ACKNOWLEDGMENTS

101 Winning Drills from the AVCA, Volume 1, is a unique collection of the finest drills gathered by the American Volleyball Coaches Association (AVCA) over a nine-year period. All drills published in this book originally appeared in *Power Tips,* the official monthly drill bulletin of the AVCA.

The project has been several years in the making and would never have materialized without the hard work of two distinguished members of the AVCA Education and Publications Committee, Don Shondell, Ph.D., and Geri Polvino, Ph.D. Shondell, who recently retired from coaching after 34 years at the helm of the Ball State University men's volleyball program, is a 1996 inductee into the Volleyball Hall of Fame, a recipient of the AVCA Founders Award in 1996 and is the second-winningest coach in NCAA men's volleyball history, behind UCLA's Al Scates (more than 700 wins). Shondell, in retirement, still enjoys his post as physical education professor at Ball State. Polvino also retired recently after 32 years at the helm of the Eastern Kentucky University women's volleyball program. Polvino is one of the world's first certified female FIVB coach instructors and has earned more than 600 career victories at Eastern Kentucky. Polvino is also a member of the USA Volleyball Coaching Accreditation Program (CAP) Cadre.

In addition, a hearty thanks goes out to the 92 volleyball coaches who originally submitted their drills to *Power Tips* and shared their knowledge and love for the game with others. Their willingness to advance the sport through shared experience is greatly appreciated and instrumental to the growth of the sport.

Finally, many thanks go to Tom Bast and everyone else at Coaches Choice for their inveterate support and expertise.

Kinda S. Lenberg
AVCA Director of Publications
December, 1999

CONTENTS

In May 1990, the executive director of the American Volleyball Coaches Association (AVCA), Sandra L. Vivas, stated in the premiere issue of *Power Tips*, "Our ongoing commitment is the advancement and development of volleyball. This begins at the high school and junior club levels, and we believe *Power Tips* can help us achieve this objective."

Power Tips, now in its ninth year, is the official drill bulletin of the AVCA. It is a publication geared specifically toward a high school/club coach audience; however, collegiate coaches also reap the benefit of its content, including articles about technique and strategy, psychology of sport, nutrition, etc., as well as three new volleyball drills every month.

Since 1990, the AVCA has gathered more than 300 drills which have appeared in *Power Tips* —drills that have been submitted by such coaching greats as Russ Rose (head women's volleyball coach, Penn State University), Lisa Love (former head women's volleyball coach and current associate athletics director at the University of Southern California), Don Shaw (head women's volleyball coach, Stanford University), and Sue Gozansky (head women's volleyball coach at the University of California–Riverside). In 1999, with the help of Don Shondell, Ph.D. (former head men's volleyball coach at Ball State University) and Geri Polvino, Ph.D. (former head women's volleyball coach at Eastern Kentucky University), the AVCA and Coaches Choice have gleaned the 101 best drills from 92 coaches to add to your collection. These drills have been carefully chosen and grouped into the following nine categories:

1. Beginning-Level Drills
2. Conditioning Drills
3. Serving/Passing Drills
4. Pass/Hit/Block Drills
5. Attacking Drills
6. Setting Drills
7. Transition Drills
8. Team Offense Drills
9. Defense Drills

Take some time to explore *101 Winning Drills form the AVCA, Volume 1*. This voluminous collection is sure to provide an excellent resource for any coach, contributing new ideas on old drill themes or offering just the right activity for your next practice.

For more information on the monthly publication *Power Tips*, contact the AVCA office at (719) 576-7777, ext. 102.

INTRODUCTION

Stephanie Schleuder, in her book *Comprehensive Volleyball Statistics: A Guide for Coaches, Media and Fans* (available through the AVCA by calling 719-576-7777, ext. 102), offers some excellent suggestions for coaches either to develop their own drills or to utilize those constructed by others:

"Many beginning coaches do not realize that the best drills they can use are those made up specifically for their own teams. Drill concepts can be borrowed from other coaches, but rarely will one coach's drill be designed to meet the specific needs of another person's team."

As a result, coaches who are looking to develop their own drills should "define the specific problem area; set up a practice situation which is similar to the game situation where the problem occurs; outline the problem for the team, giving the players a solution or way to solve it; set expectations or goals for the team; and evaluate the team performance and get player feedback" (Schleuder, 1998).

The drills found in this collection will not only provide a coach with insight into how to challenge players during practice, but they will also give the coach a solid repertoire of time-tested exercises. The coach should then be able to modify each drill in the collection to fit the specific needs of his or her team.

Each drill in this publication follows the same formula:

- Drill number and title

- Number of players necessary to perform the drill

- Number of balls necessary to perform the drill

- Drill objective (explains the purpose of the drill and what skills are being highlighted)

- Directions (how to set up the drill and run it through to the end)

Some drills provide scoring directions, while others offer suggestions for variations, depending on the players' skill levels. Accompanying each set of directions is a graphic representation of the drill, laid out on a typical volleyball court, complete with arrows showing player and ball movement (as well as a diagram key to determine player positions). In addition, there is a terminology glossary to help beginning coaches with some of the more obscure volleyball terms that may be utilized in a particular drill.

CHAPTER 1

BEGINNING-LEVEL DRILLS

DRILL #1: BLIND RECEPTION

Number of Players: 2

Number of Balls: 12

Objective: To develop the athlete's quickness, reaction and recovery time, as well as communication skills.

Directions:

1. Drape a blanket across the middle of the net, as shown in the diagram.

2. The coach (C) tosses one ball at a time to the two receiving players (P1, P2).

3. Balls may be tossed deep, short, and side to side.

4. Balls may be tossed as rapidly as deemed necessary.

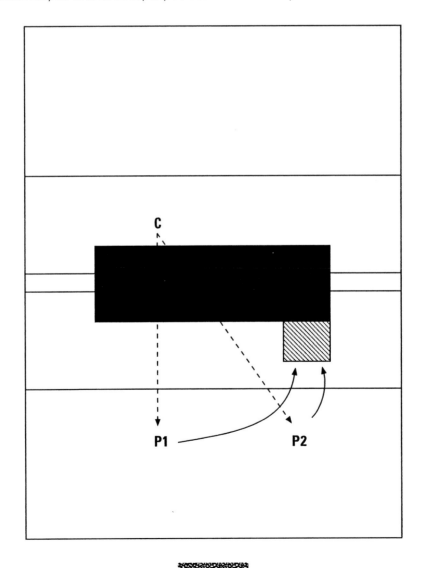

DRILL #2: FREEZE THREES

Number of Players: 6–8

Number of Balls: 10 or more

Objective: To force players to focus on platform control and ball contact on defense in a competitive situation.

Directions:

1. The coach (C) initiates the drill by hitting a ball (preferably from across the net) at three deep defenders (X1-X3, P1-P3). The player digging the ball must freeze his or her platform and look at it after contact with the ball while counting "1-1,000" loud enough for C to hear.

2. The ball is played out in three vs. three or four vs. four play (optional fourth player is a setter [S] on each side).

3. Each first contact in the rally requires the player to follow the "freeze" rules described above.

4. The rally ends immediately if a player does not meet the "freeze" requirement; otherwise, it continues until its natural conclusion, following normal volleyball rules (players may be allowed to hit front row or be limited to back row only). The team winning the rally scores a point.

5. For the next rally, C brings the ball in to the opposite team. Rally score is kept to 15, with teams switching sides at eight so that each faces C as both a right-side and a left-side attacker.

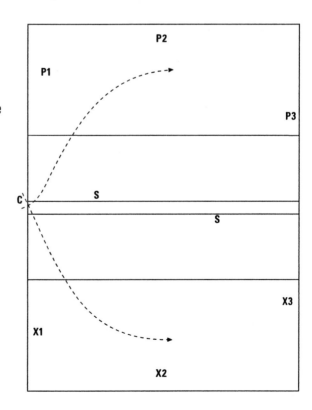

DRILL #3: LUNCH COVERAGE

Number of Players: 9 or more

Number of Balls: 10

Objective: To improve coverage off the block. Players learn to dig lower and more quickly. There is an inherent intensity whereby no ball falls, no matter how hard the block.

Directions:

1. The coach (C) tosses a free ball to a regular six-person team (X).

2. Blockers (B) are at the net, holding a school lunch tray, and the hitters hit into the block.

3. Teams must cover and dig every ball. (The velocity of the ball coming off the tray makes a game situation come very easily.)

DRILL #4: NARROW COURT TWO-ON-TWO GAMES

Number of Players: 4

Number of Balls: 1

Objective: To stress the use of the overhand pass and set. It is a great drill to develop the skills of young players.

Directions:

1. Players compete in a game-like situation, with three hits on a side (no spiking). The court is 15 feet wide and 10 feet deep or 10 feet wide and 10 feet deep. (Tape must be added to define interior sidelines [see diagram].)

Variations:

1. The court can be divided in half by length.

2. Scoring can be switched to rally.

3. The ball can be put in play with a toss or a serve from a player or a coach.

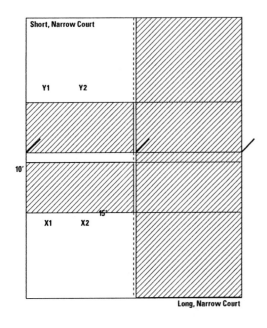

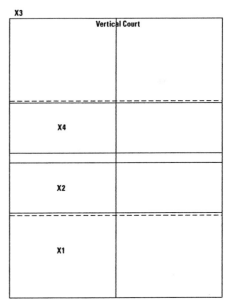

DRILL #5: NET PEPPER

Number of Players: 1

Number of Balls: 1

Objective: To encourage solid ball control and to provide a good cardiovascular workout for individual players.

Directions:

1. One player (X) passes, sets and hits to himself/herself, using the volleyball net as a partner. The key is to hit the bottom of the net so the ball pops out, then use a "j" stroke to get the ball up. To increase difficulty and emphasize movement, have the players hit side to side.

2. The player peppers for a set amount of time.

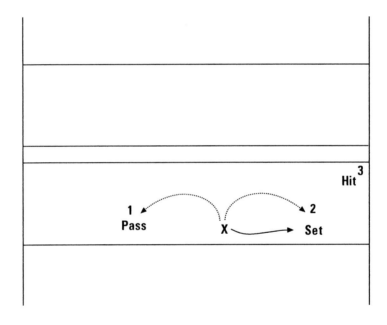

DRILL #6: OFFENSIVE COVER

Number of Players: 9

Number of Balls: 6 or more

Objective: This drill stresses covering hitters each time and works on getting a second attack if there is a block.

Directions:

1. Three coach/players (C/P) with a ball each stand on a stable platform. On cue, C/P holds the ball over the net.

2. The opposing hitter (H) approaches, jumps and swings while the team gets into offensive cover positions.

3. C/P releases or pushes the ball as the hitter swings (or shortly thereafter).

4. All hitters transition and the setter (S) sets away from the previous block.

5. The team covers again.

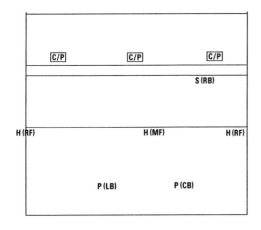

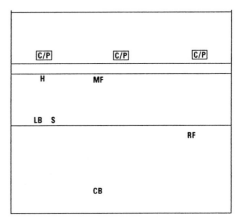

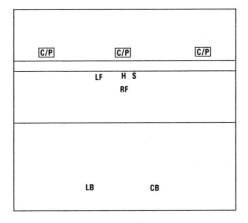

DRILL #7: OVER-THE-NET PEPPER

Number of Players: 12

Number of Balls: 13

Objective: To utilize a more game-like version of traditional pepper to warm up the players adequately, helping the hitters develop line and cut options and teaching the digger to learn to read those actions.

Directions:

1. Move the antennae in to create three separate narrow court boundaries (see diagram).

2. Position three teams of four players each (X) on the court. Begin the drill with standing spiking and then move to jumping and hitting.

3. Remind the players to hit both line and cut shots over the net, not just the usual "facing the digger" shots.

Scoring:

1. The number of net crossings calculates scoring. The group with the highest score of three-hits-in-a-row net crossings is declared the winner.

Variations:

1. The drill also works well with three players per team, with the setter at the net ducking back and forth for both sides.

2. The diggers/hitters can swap after every net crossing to help players move more.

3. The coach can increase the challenge by defining what an attack is: (a) low level—simply control the ball; (b) medium level—standing spike to jumping and spiking; (c) high level—aggressive hitting only.

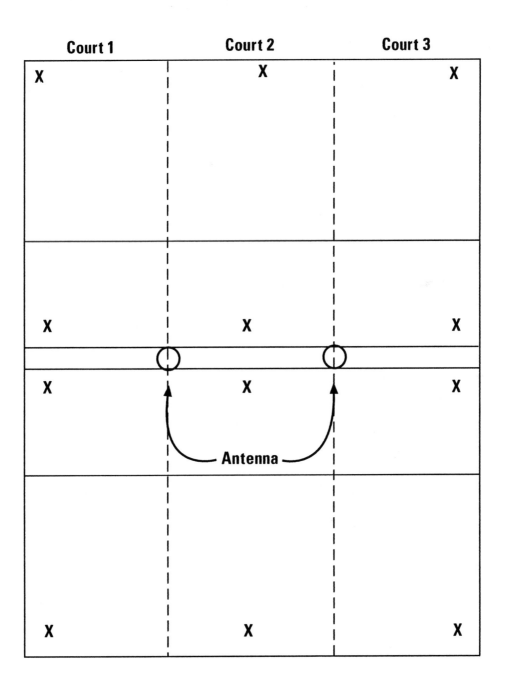

Court 1   Court 2   Court 3

Antenna

DRILL #8: RUN-THROUGH TRIPLES

Number of Players: 8–14

Number of Balls: 20

Objective: To encourage better ball control on defense, improving communication and aggressiveness.

Directions:

1. On the court, six players are set up in back-court defensive positions (X). Players are encouraged to start defense deep.

2. The coach (C) initiates the ball from the sideline. The players play the ball out using roll shots and tips high enough to clear a block.

3. Players must stay on their feet, run through the ball and, if necessary, bend their elbows at the point of contact with the ball to keep it on their side of the net. (Players must stay behind the 25-foot line before the ball is hit.)

4. When the ball is attacked, the players release, communicate, and play the ball. They must then return to their deep defensive positions and continue the rally. The losing team goes off and the winning team stays on.

Scoring:

1. The score is kept by counting the number of wins. A game goes to 15 points.

Variations:

1. Have the players complete 30 good run-through digs before they are out of the drill.

2. Have the setter (S) set both teams, changing sides with each transition under the net.

3. Use no setter at the net. Each team must set for itself.

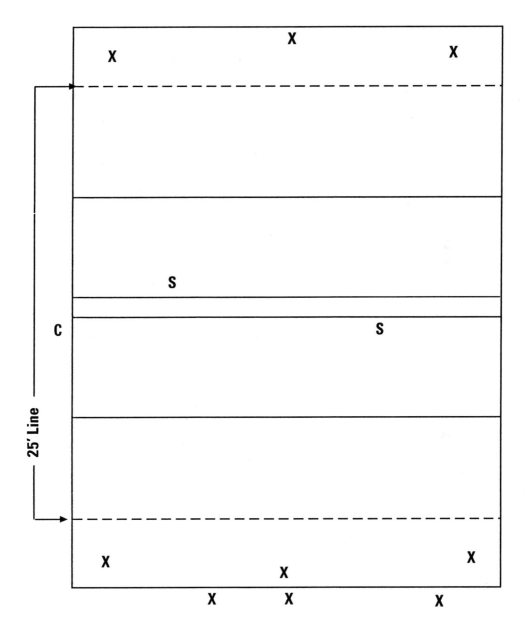

DRILL #9: SECOND CONTACT BY NON-SETTERS

Number of Players: 12

Number of Balls: Steady supply

Objective: This is a multi-purpose drill initiated with a focus on non-setters setting high, outside sets. The ability to get a good swing at the ball is a team goal and everyone should be accountable for its outcome. The coach is able to isolate one overhead passer, one hitter, etc., and provide response opportunities that are random and sequential.

Directions:

1. The coach (C) sets up two teams of six players each (P, X).

2. C tosses the ball to one side, representing the first contact. The ball is played until its termination and a point is awarded. The next toss is to the opposing team, alternating to even out the opportunities to score a point.

3. The first team to score 15 (and is ahead by two points) wins.

Variations:

1. Design your own scoring system.

2. Play the starters against the rest of the team or the varsity vs. the junior varsity. If it is a "first team/second team" drill, make sure the first team focuses on repetitions of high, outside sets from setters and non-setters. Use a scrimmage situation with feedback on the specific skill of overhead passing and its possible effect on play. Make sure the second team uses the opportunity to work on defense vs. limited attack options. Limited options handicap the first team and allow for an extremely competitive scrimmage.

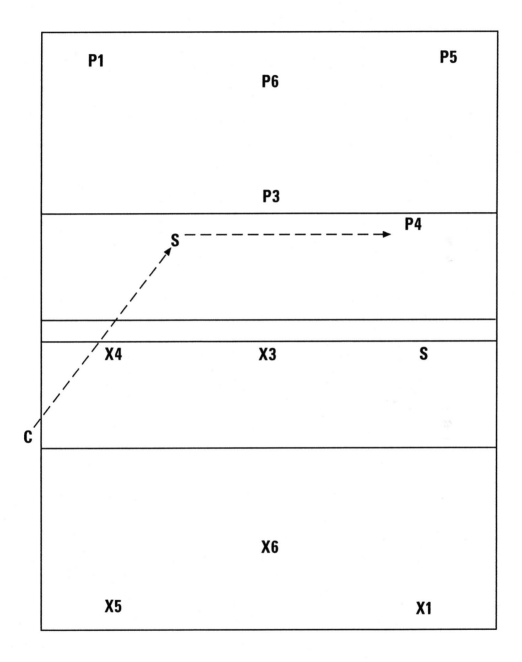

DRILL #10: SIMON SAYS "VOLLEYBALL"

Number of Players: 6

Number of Balls: 0

Objective: To teach the JV and varsity the changing positions necessary to compete at a higher level.

Directions:

1. The team begins in basic starting positions.

2. The coach (C) yells, "Simon says serve receive," and players must run to serve receive and hold basic stances.

3. C yells, "Simon says basic defense; right-side defense; middle or left." C can mix it up without saying, "Simon says," whereby players must stand in the previous position. If someone moves, then the entire team must run, do push-ups, sprint, do sit-ups, etc.

Simon Says Start Basic Positions

X1	X6	S^2
$S^{1/X2}$	X3	X4

Simon Says Serve Receive

X1	**X6**
$S^{1/X2}$ **X3**	S^2
	X4

Simon Says Basic Defense

	X1
S^2	**X6**
S^1 **X3**	**X4**

DRILL #11: SWITCH FAST FOR FREE BALL

Number of Players: 9–15

Number of Balls: Steady supply

Objective: This drill is beneficial to the JV programs in schools where there are a lot of overpasses. The drill encourages players to switch quickly to position after the serve, if there is an overpass, and is good preparation against a team that is not strong and tries to pass the ball over quickly.

Directions:

1. Set up six players on the serving side (X) and three to six players on the receiving side (P), plus ball retrievers.

2. X1 serves the ball to the passers (P), who quickly pass the ball over from the serve.

3. As a result, the serving team is forced to switch positions quickly. The serving team must then play the ball to target or set and hit.

4. The coach (C) can also hit the ball as soon as the server's ball comes over the net to the position the server is playing.

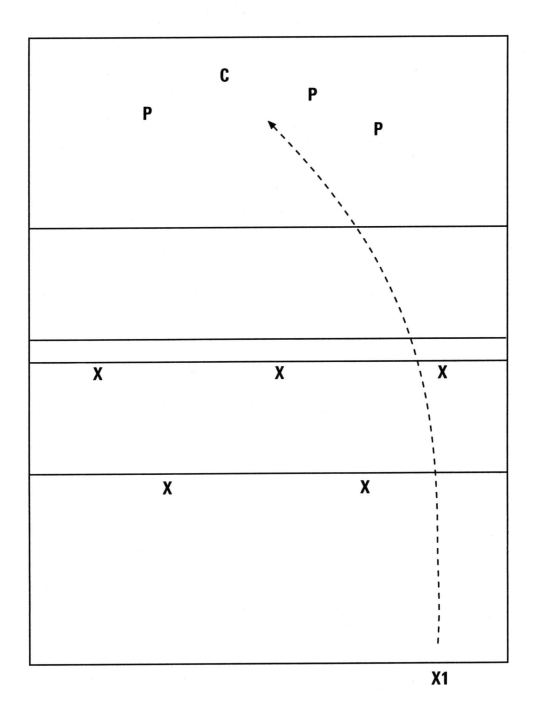

DRILL #12: TEAM DOUBLES HALF-COURT DEEP HIT

Number of Players: 10–14

Number of Balls: Steady supply

Objective: To encourage players to realize immediately the rewards of good defense. A player who executes a good dig is immediately rewarded with an attack opportunity. The drill can be used in practices at the beginning to set the tone for an intense and competitive practice and/or as a fast-paced, competitive and fun way to end a practice on a high note.

Directions:

1. Two players (P) from each team are on the court, while the remaining players on each team wait behind their own end line.

2. Play is initiated by the coach (C1), who attacks or hits off-speed to the "A" court.The two players on the court for Team A attempt to dig, set and attack for a kill.

3. The player from Team A deep hits the ball over the net (whether via attack or free ball and whether the ball lands in or out), quickly exits the court and is immediately replaced by the first player from Team A waiting in line. The player who exits then goes to the back of Team A's line.

4. Meanwhile, play continues, with Team B attempting to dig Team A's attack, then setting and deep hitting for a kill. The player from Team B who sends the ball over the net is immediately replaced, as with Team A.

5. After the rally is terminated, Coach 2 (C2) immediately initiates play for the next rally with either an attack or an off-speed shot to Team B and then the rally is played out.

Scoring:

1. Use rally scoring. Play mini-games to eight or 10 points, the best of five games. Put tape down for the attack line at 5, 7.5, or 10 feet.

```
                    P12              Team A        P14
                    P11                            P13
        ┌───────────────────────────┬───────────────────────────┐
        │                           │                           │
        │                           │                           │
        │      P3         P4        │      P5         P6        │
        │                           │                           │
        │                           │                           │
        ├───────────────────────────┼───────────────────────────┤
        │                           │                           │
   C1   ├───────────────────────────┼───────────────────────────┤   C2
        │                           │                           │
        │                           │                           │
        ├───────────────────────────┼───────────────────────────┤
        │                           │                           │
        │      P1         P2        │      P7         P8        │
        │                           │                           │
        └───────────────────────────┴───────────────────────────┘
                    P9               Team B        P15
                    P10                            P16
```

DRILL #13: THREE-STEP, TWO-STEP BLOCK

Number of Players: 6 or more

Number of Balls: 5 or more

Objective: This drill is used to work on blocker footwork and movement across the net.

Directions:

1. One player (X1) hits the ball to the top of the net. The blocker (B) blocks and slides to X3 and blocks.

2. B then slides to X2 and blocks. The pattern continues through X4, X3, X5 and back to X4.

3. Have the hitters (X1–X5) tap the ball before the hit so B can establish a rhythm.

4. B goes to X5, X5 to X4, etc. X1 becomes B or gets in the blocking line. (The managers [M] are used to keep the balls off the court.)

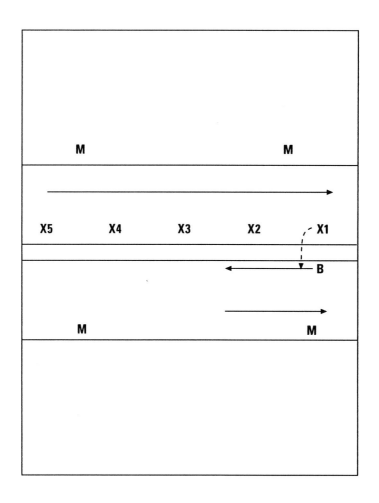

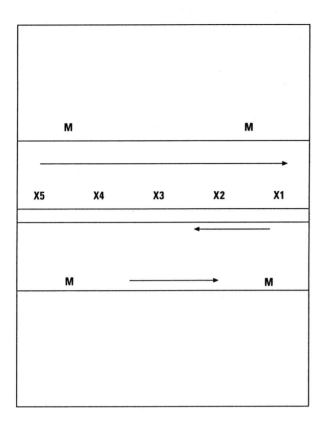

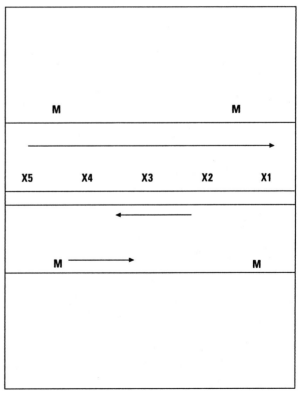

DRILL #14: TIP GAME

Number of Players: 4

Number of Balls: 1

Objective: This is a simple drill to develop ball control, work on tipping skills and to foster communication among players.

Directions:

1. Set up two teams of two players (X, P) on each side of the net.

2. Tape off three 10' x 10' courts (see diagram).

3. The server (X1) serves from the 3-meter line.

4. P1 and P2 play the ball out, with all volleyball rules applying, except players attack by tipping.

5. Play a game to 11; a team must win by two points.

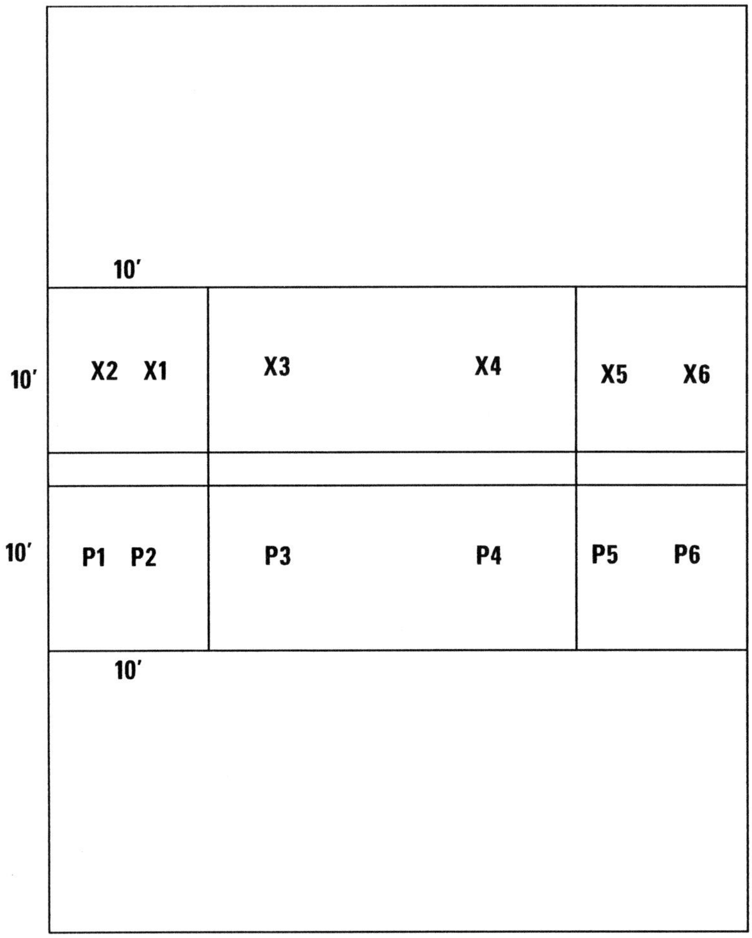

10'				
X2 X1	**X3**	**X4**	**X5**	**X6**
P1 P2	**P3**	**P4**	**P5**	**P6**
10'				

10' (left side vertical labels for the X row and P row)

CHAPTER 2

CONDITIONING DRILLS

DRILL #15: CROSS-COUNTRY CONDITIONING

Number of Players: 8–12

Number of Balls: 4-6

Objective: This is a high-intensity drill involving the skills of digging, attacking, blocking and running.

Directions:

1. The coaches (C1 and C2) tip or spike to players (X1 and X4) for a dig.

2. After a successful dig, X1 and X4 approach and swing.

3. After a swing, X1 and X4 cross over to mock block MF and LF.

4. After blocking, X1 and X4 turn and dive, roll, or sprawl.

5. X1 and X4 sprint to the other side of the court and begin again.

6. Repeat as many times as desired, according to the conditioning level of the athletes.

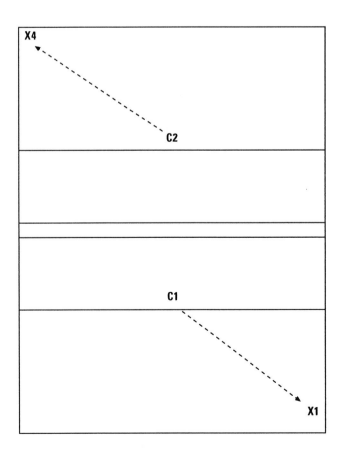

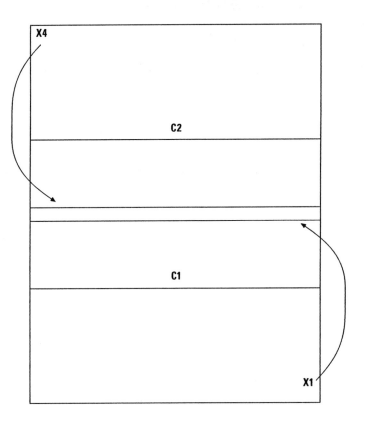

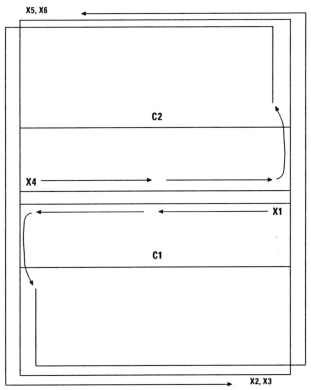

DRILL #16: DEFENSIVE CIRCUIT

Number of Players: 2 per side

Number of Balls: 6–8 per side

Objective: To develop quickness and stamina.

Directions:

1. Player X1 begins the drill, starting in Position A.

2. One coach (C1) hits the ball down the line to X1 in Position A.

3. After playing the ball, X1 shifts to each other position as indicated:

    B—dink   C—deep corner back

    D—tip   E—deep crosscourt

4. C2 continues the drill, spiking to X1 in position F.

5. Finally, C2 sets a deep set at Position G, with X1 attacking crosscourt.

Variation:

1. This drill can be run with two or three players going through the circuit at intervals, thus keeping the drill moving at a continuous pace. Each additional player added to the drill should be incorporated after the preceding player has gotten past Position E.

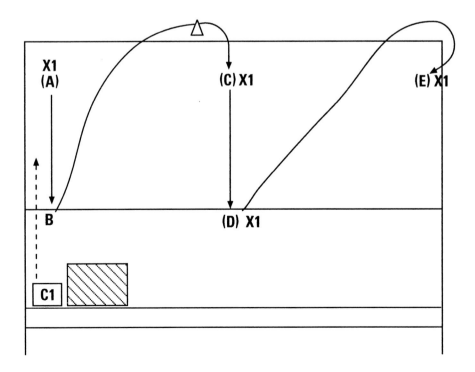

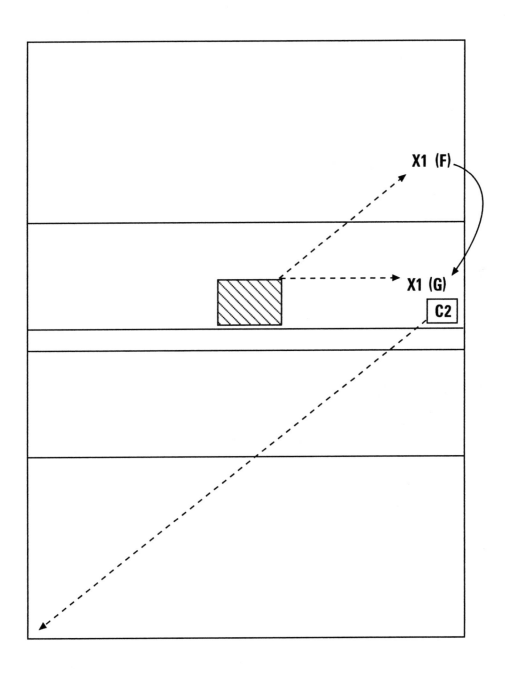

X1 (F)

X1 (G)

C2

DRILL #17: FOUR-ON-FOUR CONTINUOUS PLAY

Number of Players: 12

Number of Balls: Steady supply

Objective: Since there are only four players, the athletes involved in this drill get many opportunities to play the ball. It incorporates conditioning into the drills and the continuous action helps maintain a high level of intensity.

Directions:

1. Divide the teams into three groups of four. One group is off to the side doing three sets of one-minute circuits (jump rope, medicine ball, push-ups, etc.). The other two groups play four-on-four.

2. Coaches (C1, C2) stand off to the side on each side of the net with balls.

3. Play begins when Team A serves. Play continues until the ball is down on one side of the net. If the ball is down on Team A's side, C1 throws a free ball over the net to Team B. The coaches continue to send free balls or hard-driven hits at the end of each rally. The drill is timed for three minutes. Rotate one team to circuits.

Variations:

1. C1 serves to Team B when the ball is down on Team A's side.

2. C1 puts the ball into play on Team A's side (only have two hits remaining).

3. A team rotates every time the ball goes over the net.

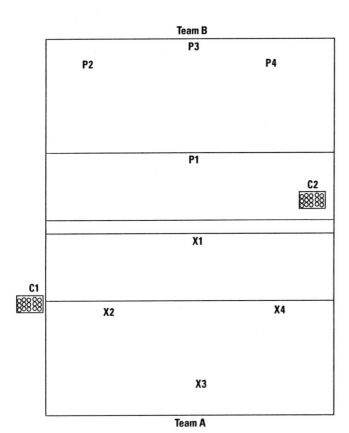

Team B

P3

P2   P4

P1

C2

X1

C1

X2   X4

X3

Team A

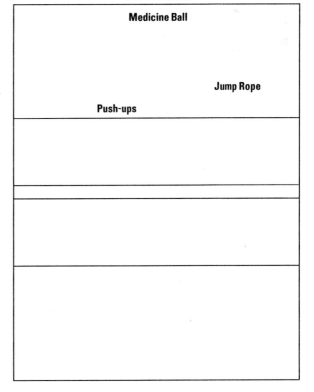

Team C Stations

Medicine Ball

Jump Rope

Push-ups

DRILL #18: GIANT ROTATION PASSING

Number of Players: 8 or more

Number of Balls: Steady supply

Objective: This drill incorporates cardiovascular training into the practice program while still keeping players' hands on the volleyballs. The drill is very beneficial for the practice of passing when fatigued; it also provides numerous passing repetitions.

Directions:

1. Coaches (C) on each side of the net serve to the passers (P).

2. Passers, catchers (CR), and feeders (F) rotate by sprinting to the next position.

3. The drill continues for 20–30 minutes.

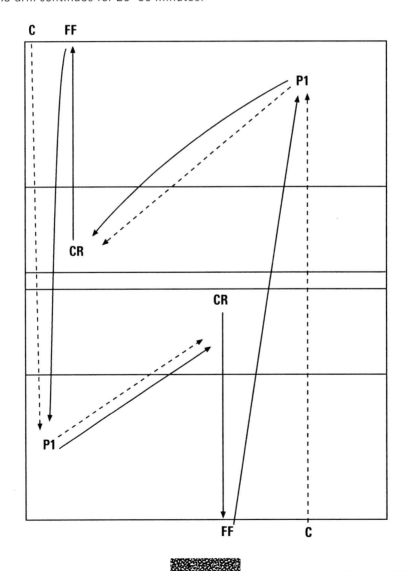

CHAPTER 3

SERVING/PASSING DRILLS

DRILL #19: 15-POINT SERVING/PASSING GAME

Number of Players: 12

Number of Balls: Steady supply

Objective: To provide a fast-paced serve and receive situation. The winner is the individual who first scores 15 points. This drill should move along quickly, and servers should serve at a fast rate, while passers need to rotate to fill the court after every serve.

Directions:

1. The drill begins with three passers on the court (P1, P2, and P3) and two other passers (P4 and P5) waiting beside the receiving end. All other players are lined up in the service area.

2. Passers move one position to the right after every serve, even if a serving error occurs.

3. A coach (C) is positioned in the target area and decides whether the pass counts for a point. If so, the player receiving the point calls out his/her current count. If the passer is aced, he/she exchanges places with the server who aced him/her.

4. Passers must immediately fill the gap vacated by the person who was aced. The service ace also counts as a point, so the server updates his/her score out loud. Ace serves must always be counted against someone so that numbers in the lines remain constant.

5. A pass or serve can also be judged as being in the "just OK" category so that neither player leaves his/her area.

6. When someone reaches 15 points, the drill is over.

Penalties:

1. To encourage a high percentage of good serves, penalize servers when they miss. A ball that hits the net results in an immediate lap around the court and the penalty for a long serve is five sit-ups before getting back in line to serve.

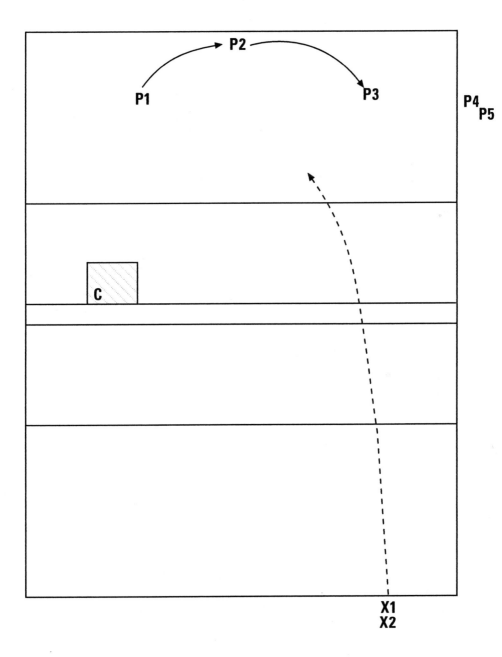

DRILL #20: + - 0 SHORT SERVE AND RUN

Number of Players: 12

Number of Balls: 12

Objective: To develop short serving practice and to foster concentration on the skill. The drill gives immediate feedback to the players when the ball is on or inside the 3-meter line. It creates pressure and team focus on the task at hand.

Directions:

1. Players (P) line up behind opposite end lines to serve. They are attempting to serve on the 3-meter line or just inside of it.

2. Each player serves the ball and is given a score of +1 for a ball inside the colored area, a zero when the ball is elsewhere in the court, and a -1 for a serving error.

3. The player jogs to the opposite side of the court to repeat the sequence.

4. The goal of each server is to reach +10.

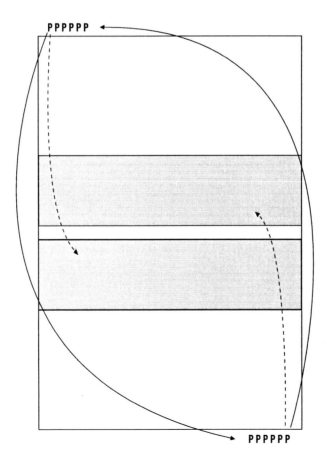

DRILL #21: ACE TO WIN

Number of Players: 12

Number of Balls: 1 or more

Objective: To increase players' abilities to serve aggressively and pass efficiently in "game point" situations. In executing this drill, the weakest servers often drill a ball over the net, as well as strategically place a ball into areas of weakness. Serve reception is greatly improved, as there is little to no hesitation going for the ball; communication is heightened; and rallies are filled with aggressive hitting and quick movement to "save" a flailing ball.

Directions:

1. Set up two teams of six players (X, P) in regularly assigned playing positions.

2. The coach (C) designates a random total score (e.g., the first team to three points wins). Any number of points may be chosen, but beware—if the play is intense, reaching three to five points in less than an hour can be quite difficult.

3. The rules are simple: (1) a point can only be scored on a service ace; (2) a team can only gain possession of the ball through either a side out or a point. It is very important to determine what constitutes a "service ace" at the start in order to overcome any discrepancies that may occur throughout the drill.

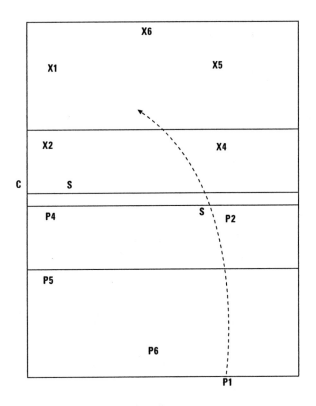

DRILL #22: MINIATURE GOLF SERVING—NINE HOLES

Number of Players: 12

Number of Balls: 12

Objective: To work on spot serving and conditioning, in addition to demanding server concentration when transitioning from the front row to the back row in a game situation.

Directions:

1. Line up six players on Net 1 at the service line (Group 1) and six on Net 2 at the service line (Group 2).

2. Each server has a ball—one behind the other at the service line.

3. Coach 1 and Coach 2 (C1, C2) record results on a notepad or have players keep score.

4. To begin, Server 1 (P1) and Server 7 (P7) serve to Hole or Position 1, then sprint to retrieve the ball. If the ball hits the immediate area, then one point is scored. If not, no points are scored. After ball retrieval is finished, the server lines up at the opposite service line.

5. When P1 and P7 complete the serve, P2 and P8 position themselves to serve on line.

6. Once set, the servers serve to Hole 1 also, then sprint immediately after controlled release.

7. This procedure continues until all six servers serve, then the group moves to Hole 2 or Position 2 until all servers serve all nine holes.

8. The coach announces the winner at the end of round No. 1 immediately following the drill or may tabulate results at each practice for a weekly or seasonal winner.

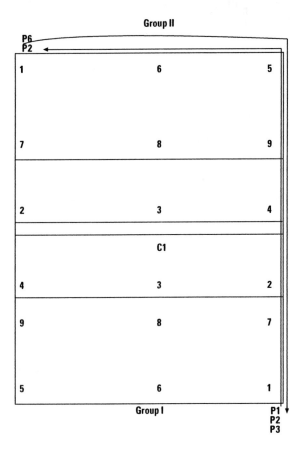

Group II

P6
P2

1	6	5
7	8	9
2	3	4

C1

4	3	2
9	8	7
5	6	1

Group I

P1
P2
P3

P12
P7

1	6	5
7	8	9
2	3	4

C2

4	3	2
9	8	7
5	6	1

P7
P8
P9

DRILL #23: PING PONG SCORING

Number of Players: 12

Number of Balls: 5

Objective: This drill is used to create a competitive, game-like serving atmosphere within the confines of practice. The drill is designed to train servers—not the technique of serving.

Directions:

1. Set up two teams for a scrimmage situation. Use a simple rally point game or match, but each server on both teams serves five balls consecutively before there is a rotation by both squads.

2. Since a point is scored on each serve, the server has to concentrate on hitting a quality serve or the other team will side out with ease, scoring at will. (The more equally matched the teams are, the more competitive this drill will be. This is, however, a great first team vs. second team drill because of the rally point scoring system. Anyone can score on each serve.)

3. Play the game to various point totals (45 works well).

4. Because there is such a low point total, there may not be a full rotation. As a result, when one game is completed, change sides and start in the rotation that just ended, using the same server who just completed his/her turn. Play can be a best-of-five match or a predetermined number of games.

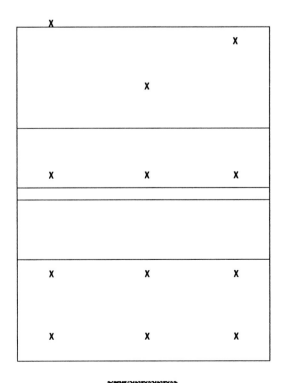

DRILL #24: SERVE AND DEFEND

Number of Players: 3–6

Number of Balls: 1 or more

Objective: To provide opportunities to practice serving, receiving, setter deep tipping and defense by the server.

Directions:

1. The server (SV) serves a ball to the receivers (P).

2. The ball is passed to the setter (S), who attempts to dump the ball over the net behind the 3-meter line.

3. SV comes on to the court to play defense.

Scoring:

1. The server gets three points for an ace.

2. One point is earned if SV touches the setter's dump.

3. Two points are earned if SV brings up the dump so that a second player could set the ball.

4. Receivers get a point each time the setter's dump lands behind the 3-meter line in-bounds, untouched.

5. SV loses two points for a missed serve and loses three points if a serve is passed over the net and lands in the court behind the 3-meter line untouched.

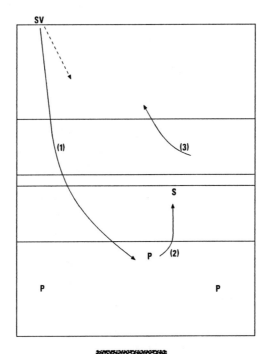

DRILL #25: SERVE AND RUN FOREVER

Number of Players: 8–16

Number of Balls: 12 or more

Objective: To entice players to practice serving tough serves after running a sprint.

Directions:

1. Attach elastic tautly from one antenna to the other, 8 inches down from the top (2 feet above the net).

2. Divide the team in half. The first player on each team runs from the end line to the 3-meter line and back four times and then serves one ball.

3. The second person in line starts running up and back when the first person has finished the second "up and back."

4. The team scores +1 for each serve under or touching the elastic; 0 for a serve over the elastic; and -1 for an error. The first team to 30 wins.

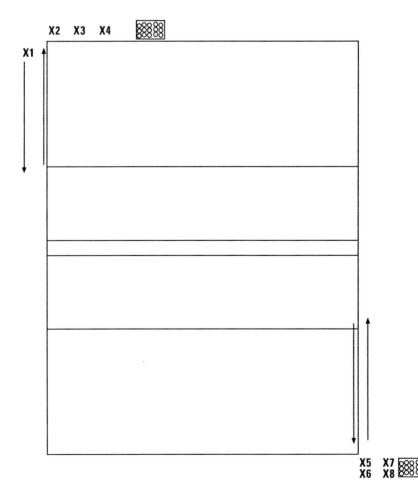

DRILL #26: SERVE PROGRESSIONS

Number of Players: 2

Number of Balls: 1

Objective: To develop serving accuracy. The technique focus should be to serve on a straight line to the target with as flat and controlled a serve as possible.

Directions:

1. Choose partners. Servers start on court and move back after they serve in two in a row.

2. Serve to the partner's waist or below.

3. The serve must pass between the net and elastic tied between the tops of the antennae.

Variation:

1. Adjust antennae to a narrower portion of the court.

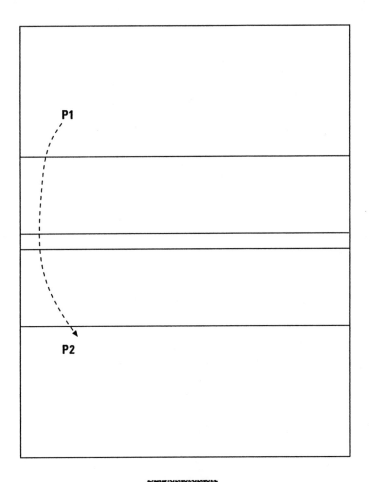

DRILL #27: SERVE/SERVE RECEIVE CHALLENGE

Number of Players: 12 or more

Number of Balls: 12 or more

Objective: This drill not only challenges passers to make perfect "ups," but also challenges servers to serve in a smart manner, as well as consistently and aggressively.

Directions:

1. Set up Team 1 in serve receive and set up Team 2 on the baseline serving.

2. The scorekeeper times five minute running time and Team 2 serves alternately at Team 1.

Scoring:

1. Team 1 scores three points for every 3 option pass (can set all options) and one point for each ball the setter can catch in an overhand passing position, but if caught outside the target area. If Team 1 is aced, 0 points are awarded.

2. Team 2 receives three points for an ace, two points for a ball caught outside the target area and -1 for a serving error.

3. After five minutes, the teams switch. The team with the highest overall score wins after a set period of time.

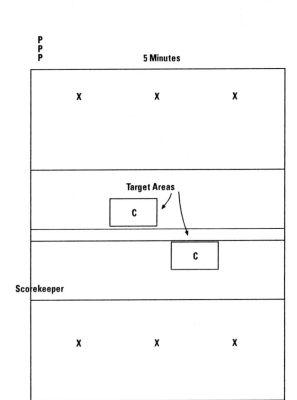

P
P
P

5 Minutes

X   X   X

Target Areas

C

C

Scorekeeper

X   X   X

P
P
P

X
X
X

5 Minutes

P   P   P

C

C

P   P   P

X
X
X

DRILL #28: SERVERS VS. PASSERS

Number of Players: 6–12

Number of Balls: 1 or more

Objective: To develop accuracy in serving and passing to target. The object of the drill is to serve tough but accurately and to pass consistently to target. The drill is excellent for encouraging competitiveness.

Directions:

1. Divide the team into two groups: servers (SV) and passers (P).

2. Servers score points with aces and serves that cannot be passed to target.

3. Passers score points when serving errors are made and when the ball is passed to target (T). Passers rotate after each serve.

4. Play the game to 15 points.

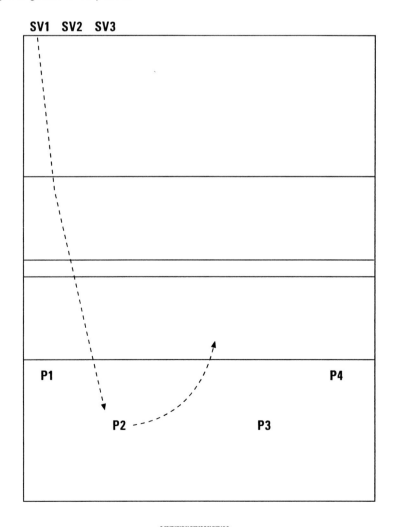

SV1   SV2   SV3

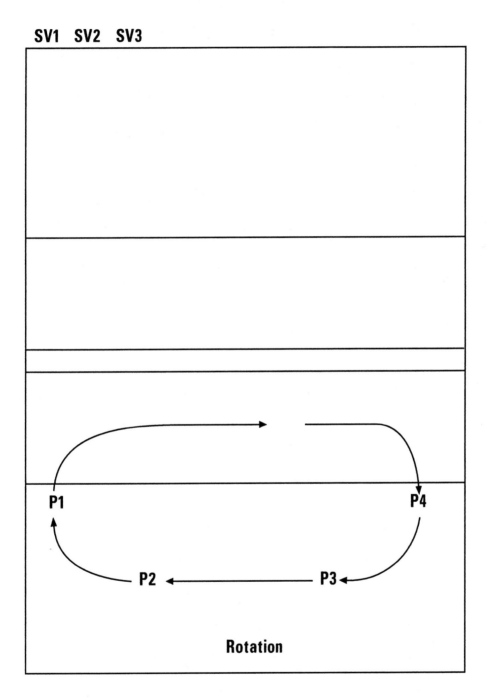

Rotation

DRILL # 29: SIDE OUT THREE TIMES TO WIN

Number of Players: 12

Number of Balls: 4

Objective: To encourages the receiving team to pass and run three successful side out plays before the serving team can serve an ace.

Directions:

1. The serving team gets five tries to serve an ace. If the team fails, the members perform sprints.

2. If the receiving team fails to run three side out plays within the five serves, then that team does the sprints. If neither team is successful, everyone runs.

3. If the receiving team is successful, those players rotate to the next serve receive formation. The serving team switches front and back row so that all of the players on the serving team get to serve.

4. The drill is completed when the receiving team has run three successful side out plays in all six rotations.

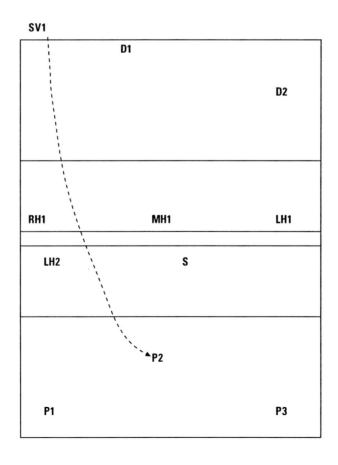

DRILL #30: SPEEDBALL/FAST GAME

Number of Players: 8–12

Number of Balls: 1 per team

Objective: To emphasize the importance of serve and serve receive.

Directions:

1. This drill can be run with doubles, triples, or quads; setters can be stationary.

2. Team A serves to Team B. Play the ball out. If Team A wins, Team C serves and tries to do it before Team A is ready. If Team B wins, Team D does the same as above.

3. The person on the losing team retrieves the ball and runs quickly to the back of the line.

4. Servers serve when the team on their side loses.

5. The first team to 10 wins. (Note: missed serves by opponents do not count.)

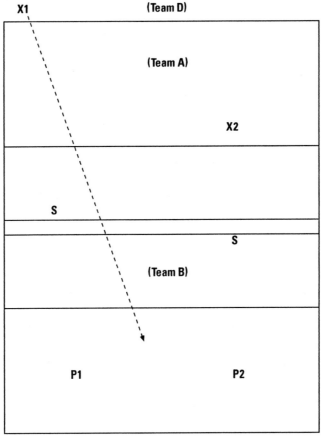

DRILL #31: TEAM SERVING GAME

Number of Players: 3–6 per side

Number of Balls: 1 per person

Objective: To provide opportunities to serve at specific targets.

Directions:

1. The coach (C) sets chairs in desired areas on the court.

2. Servers from both groups (I and II) try to hit the chair with their serves. The serve must be on the fly without a bounce.

3. The team gets a point for each serve that hits a chair (or target).

4. Players who miss two serves (or a number designated by the coach) must stop serving and sit on a chair until a teammate hits a chair with a serve.

5. All players on that side are free to serve again and start with no misses.

6. The first team to five points wins. If a team loses all its players to service errors, C can either declare the other team a winner or give the opponents one extra point and start everyone serving again.

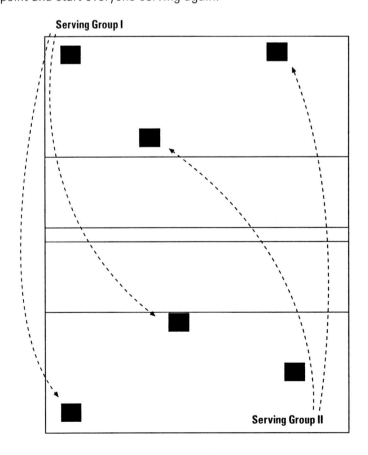

CHAPTER 4

PASS/HIT/BLOCK DRILLS

DRILL #32: ATTACKING THE OVERPASS

Number of Players: 7–10

Number of Balls: 12

Objective: To provide opportunities to practice side out offense, transitioning to base defensive positions and blockers attacking an overpass.

Directions:

1. Begin with a server (SV), three blockers (optional) and team serve receive on the other side of the net.

2. The object of the drill is to receive serve, set and attack the ball, and then immediately hit a ball that the coach (C) throws on the net, which simulates a dig that passes over the net.

3. The setter (S) can set any hitter. If the ball is blocked, keep playing until one of the players hits the ball overthrown by the coach.

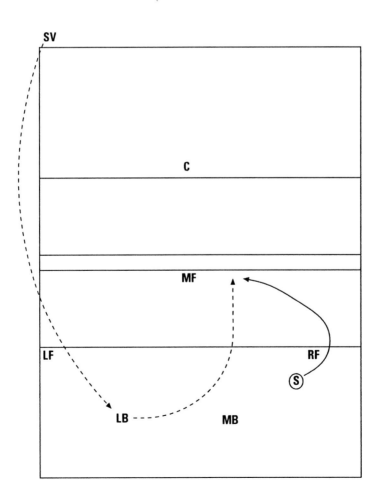

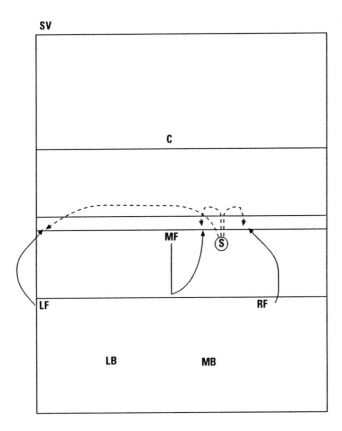

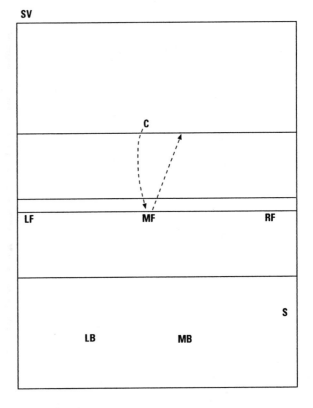

DRILL #33: BLOCK AND ATTACK IN TRANSITION

Number of Players: 8

Number of Balls: Steady supply

Objective: To prepare players for the block and transition aspect of the game. It is an excellent drill to work on the transition attack, blocking position and movement, and it improves conditioning.

Directions:

1. Set up three attackers (X) and a setter (S) on each side of the net. Have a coach (C1, C2) on each side with a cart of balls.

2. C1 tosses to S, who sets up an attack. The three front-row players on the opposite side are at the net ready to block.

3. If the ball is spiked and goes by the block, C2 on the blocker's side immediately tosses to S and the blockers quickly transition to attack readiness. The three original attackers become blockers.

4. If the ball is blocked, S on the attacker's side receives another toss and the same team attacks again.

5. The drill is continuous and can be paced for the level of players by slowing down or speeding up the time between tosses by the coaches.

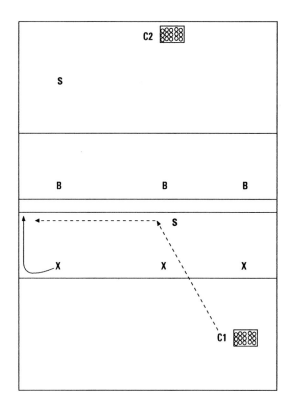

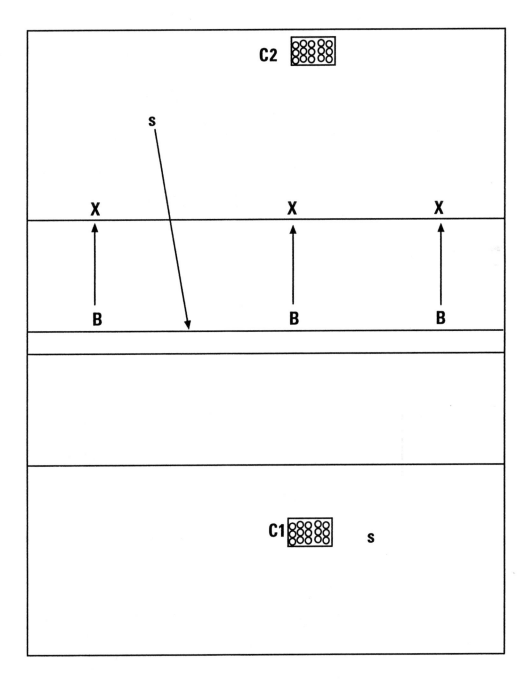

DRILL #34: BLOCK TO HIT

Number of Players: 5

Number of Balls: Steady supply

Objective: To help perfect the transition game, which requires a thorough understanding of each player's responsibilities and good communication among the players. It also requires a lot of practice in order for the skills and formations employed to be successful.

Directions:

1. Two players (LF, MF) take a blocking position vs. the coach (C) on the opposite side of the net. C will hit the ball over, around or off the blockers to a back-court digger (MB). As the digger digs to the target (T), a setter (S) will come into the front court to set the ball to one of the blockers who has quickly moved off the net into an attacking position.

2. The same blockers should stay in the drill until they have successfully completed a specified number of transition attacks.

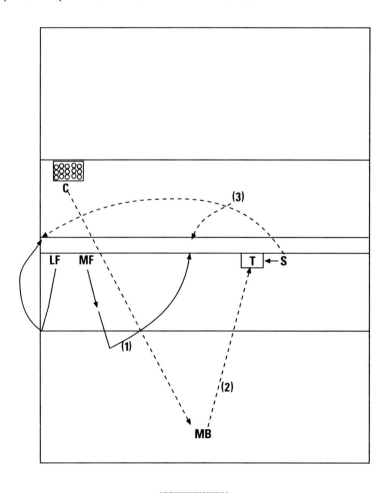

DRILL #35: BLOCK TO OFFENSE

Number of Players: 6 or more

Number of Balls: 6 or more

Objective: To provide controlled opportunities to block and convert to transition offense.

Directions:

1. The coach (C) stands on a stable platform in any hitting position.

2. In the Block Phase, C hits into the block formed by P1 and P2, who is coming from the middle position. The setter (S) moves into the appropriate position.

3. In the Transition/Attack phase, P1 and P2 come off the block and transition into the attack position. C quickly tosses a second ball to P3, who passes to S. S can go to any hitter.

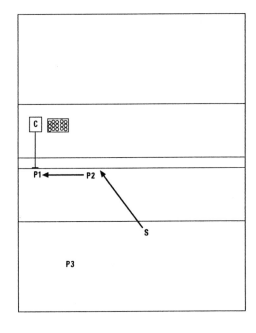

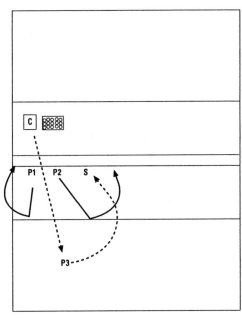

DRILL #36: LEFT SIDE VS. LEFT SIDE

Number of Players: 10

Number of Balls: 24

Objective: To encourage accuracy in hitting and digging while promoting intensity and competitiveness on the court.

Directions:

1. One coach (C1) tosses to a setter (S1).

2. S1 sets to a hitter (H1), who hits crosscourt. S2 goes up to block.

3. The digger (D1) digs the ball to S2, who sets the ball to H1.

4. H1 hits crosscourt and S1 goes up to block. As the first rally terminates, the next sequence begins with a toss by C2 on Team B's side of the net.

5. Hitters and diggers stay in the drill until they make a hitting or digging error. H2 and D2 will then be in the drill. The side that scores 15 points wins.

6. Have hitters and diggers alternate (on the same side of the court).

Scoring:

+1 = kills (a hit or tip that is crosscourt and to the left of C, who is standing in the middle)

+1 = dig (as long as the team can play the ball over the net)

+1 = block

-1 = hitting error

-1 = ball hits the floor

-1 = ball that is touched on the block, but goes to the right side of the court (this is not a kill)

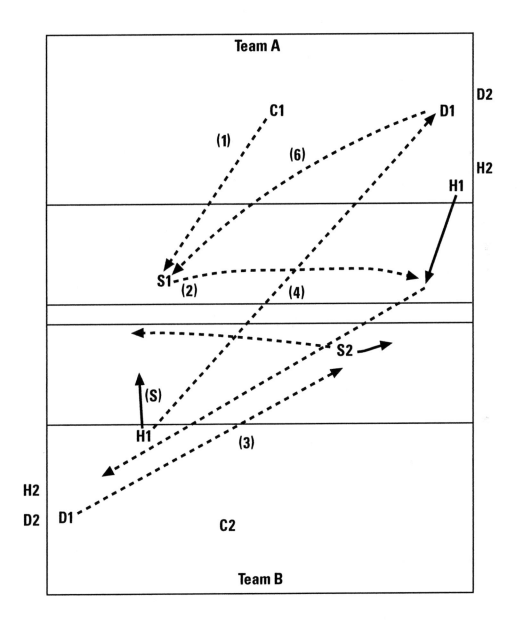

DRILL #37: OFF-BLOCK HITTING

Number of Players: 8 or more

Number of Balls: 10 or more

Objective: To teach attack transition after blocking.

Directions:

1. The coach (C) stands at the right front net target area.

2. Players in sets of three (P1, P2, P3) stand one at a time at the left front blocking position.

3. Another player (X) stands on the other side of the net on a stable platform with a ball held above the net.

4. P1 jumps, blocks the held ball and quickly gets off the net.

5. After transition, P1 digs a ball from C, then hits a tossed ball from another coach or player.

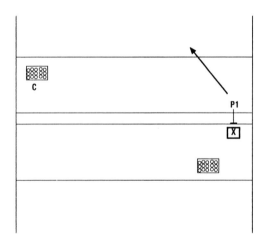

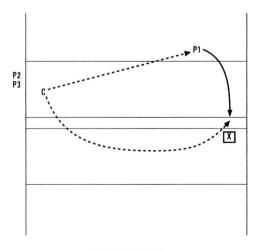

DRILL #38: ONE-MINUTE BLOCK

Number of Players: 2

Number of Balls: Steady supply

Objective: To provide multiple blocking opportunities under a controlled situation.

Directions:

1. Establish a time limit of 60 seconds. The coach (C) may determine what time is appropriate.

2. The blockers (B1, B2) attempt to block as many balls as possible from C1 and C2, who are on stable platforms.

3. The ball retrievers (X) must get the balls back into the cart and grab all loose balls.

4. Two feeders (F1, F2) are necessary.

6. The person on the platform must hit the same shot each time.

Variation:

1. Establish a time limit of 30 seconds.

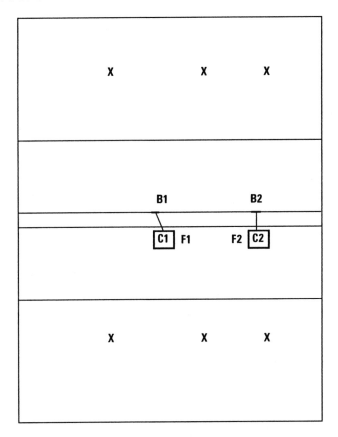

DRILL #39: QUICK VS. QUICK

Number of Players: 8

Number of Balls: 40

Objective: To convert a quick attack into a quick attack response.

Directions:

1. Each team consists of one setter (S), one quick hitter (H) and two angle diggers (LB, RB).

2. The coach (C) initiates play with a down ball to each team alternately.

3. Preferred responses include the dig, set, quick attack. Secondary responses include dig, Set A or D zone attack.

4. Rally score to five points. At five, quick attackers switch teams and play again. Points are scored only for quick attack kills or stuff blocks.

5. S does not block, but assumes defensive responsibilities at the net.

6. Wave rotation.

The Set-Up

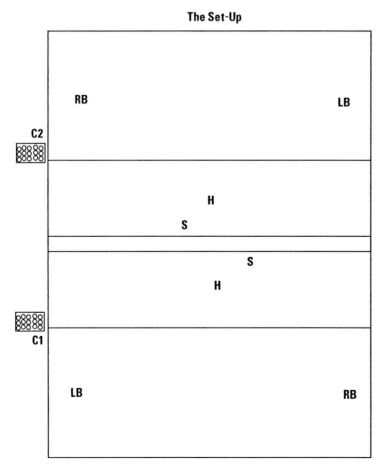

Secondary Response

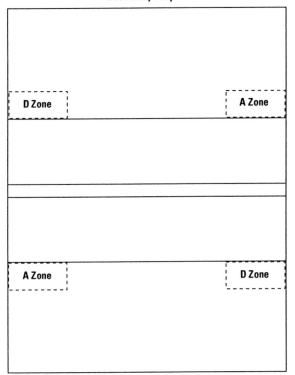

Wave Rotation

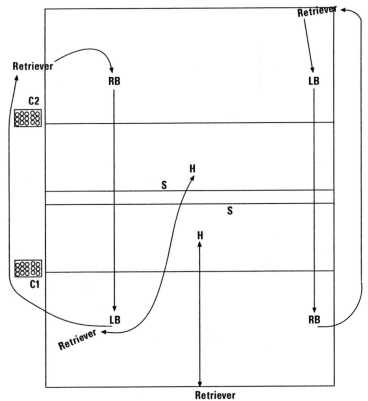

DRILL #40: PASS/HIT/BLOCK

Number of Players: 6–7

Number of Balls: 6–7

Objective: To make every part of every drill a more game-like, all-skills drill. Players must perform the basic skills of passing, hitting and blocking, while using correct footwork.

Directions:

1. The coach (C) spikes the ball to P1, who must pass to the setter (S). S sets P1 with whatever P1 calls for and hits the ball to either corner or spike rolls it into mid-court.

2. P1 hits and then goes around the post to become the blocker (B) against P2. After hitting, P2 replaces P1 at B.

3. B retrieves the ball and goes to the other side to take a place in that line.

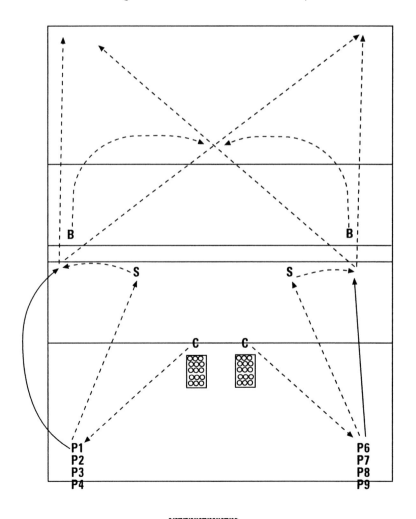

DRILL #41: READ BLOCKING

Number of Players: 6

Number of Balls: 6

Objective: To provide opportunities to work on read blocking.

Directions:

1. The coach (C) puts the ball in play.

2. One player (P) passes the ball to the setter (S).

3. S sets the ball to the outside using a variety of sets (e.g., 4 or 5 set, "d" set, back-row set).

4. Blockers (B) read the setter and block to the ball. Two or three blockers should be on the ball, depending on where the set goes.

5. Blockers must block a certain number of balls (3, 5, 7 or 10) to the floor to get out of the drill.

6. Offensive players work on coverage.

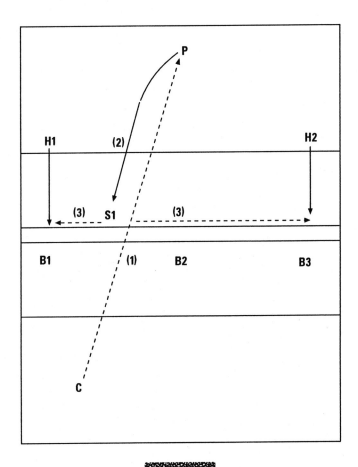

DRILL #42: READING THE HITTER

Number of Players: 6

Number of Balls: 12

Objective: To work on attacking and blocking the overpass attack.

Directions:

1. The coach (C) tosses an overset to the hitter (H).

2. The blocker (B) does not see the ball and is forced to make his/her move by watching only the hitter.

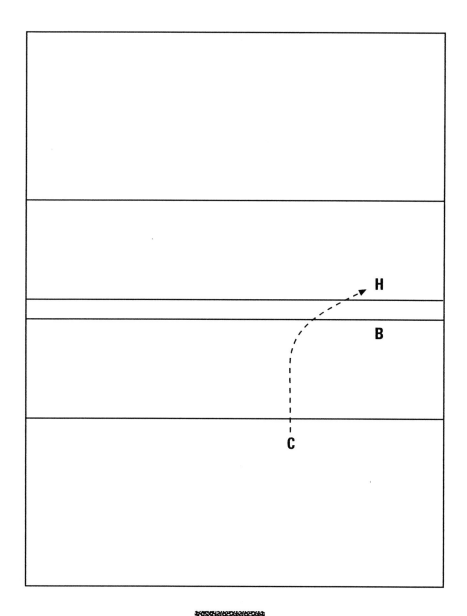

DRILL #43: SPLIT LINE HITTING VS. THREE BLOCKERS

Number of Players: 12 or more

Number of Balls: 10 or more

Objective: To involve everyone on the court; to encourage the setter to be comfortable with backsetting; and to acclimate the players to a very fast pace on the court.

Directions:

1. The coach (C) downs the ball to diggers (D) doing run-throughs.

2. D passes to the target (hitters call the set).

3. The hitters run the pattern and the setter (S) chooses whom to set.

4. The blockers (B) read and defend.

6. The hitters switch lines each time.

7. Rotate after 10 balls.

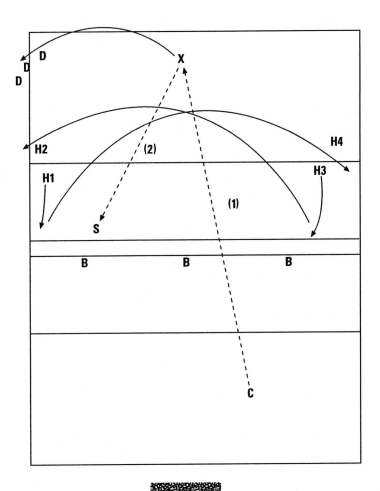

DRILL #44: THREE-BLOCK DRILL

Number of Players: 3

Number of Balls: 30

Objective: To provide blocking repetitions against a controlled attack by coaches standing on stable platforms.

Directions:

1. Three coaches (C1, C2, C3) or designated hitters stand on stable platforms positioned where the standard attack takes place.

2. The coaches hit in sequence (1–6) to the marked areas.

3. The strongside blocker (B1) works on his/her one-on-one block.

4. The middle blocker (B2) blocks one-on-one.

5. The middle blocker moves outside, using proper footwork, to the strong side blocker for a double block.

6. The sequence is then repeated with the weak side blocker (B3) and the middle blocker.

7. Coaches should hit crosscourt when hitting one-on-one, then try to hit the seam between the outside blocker and the middle blocker when hitting against a double block. The off-blocker can practice coming off the net for defense. The hitters can be positioned to simulate combinations or other sets.

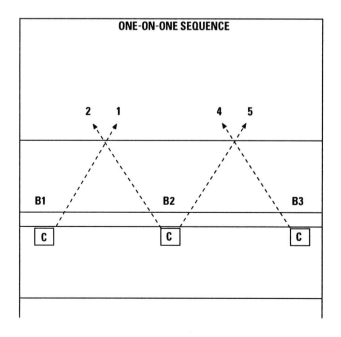

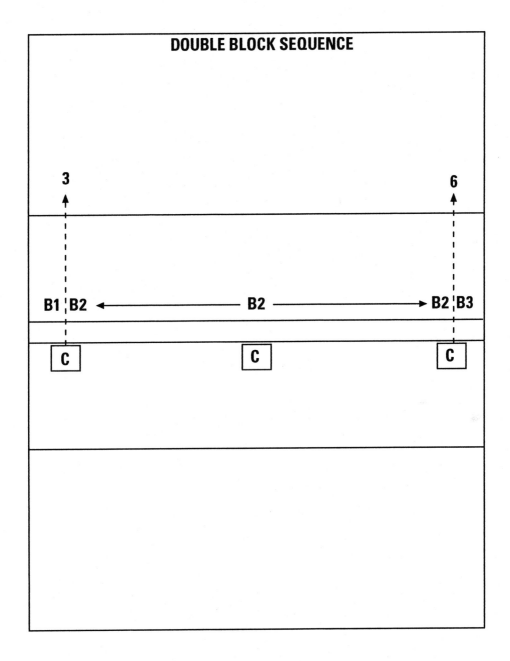

CHAPTER 5

ATTACKING DRILLS

DRILL #45: ANGLE/CROSS-COURT HITTING

Number of Players: 4–12

Number of Balls: 5–10

Objective: To encourage hitters to use the angle and crosscourt shots.

Directions:

1. The drill begins when the coach (C) tosses or hits the ball to one side of the court.

2. The players pass the ball to the setter (S), who sets the ball to the left front digger (LF).

3. The LF digger hits crosscourt to either LB or LF. Continue play until the ball is dead.

4. C tosses the ball to the side where the error occurred.

5. The person who hits rotates out. LB becomes LF and the off-court player becomes LB. The player who hit becomes the next player in.

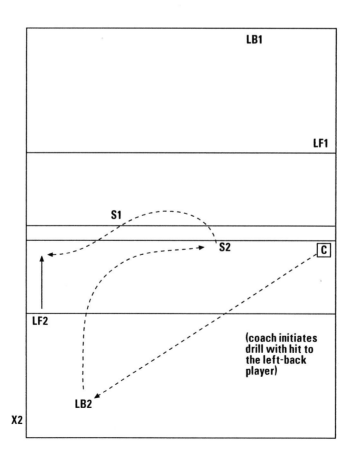

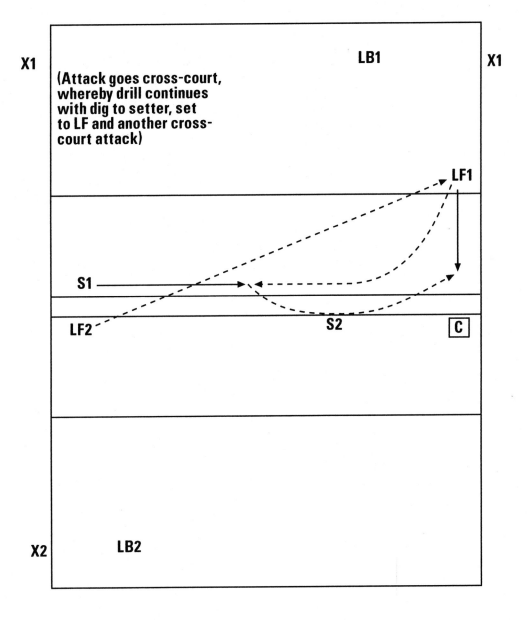

X1   **LB1**   **X1**

(Attack goes cross-court, whereby drill continues with dig to setter, set to LF and another cross-court attack)

LF1

S1

LF2   **S2**   **C**

X2   **LB2**

DRILL #46: ATTACKING THE CORNERS

Number of Players: 8–12

Number of Balls: 20 or more

Objective: To encourage players to place back-court attacks to the corners of the opponent's court. It works both offense/attacking the corners and defense/defending the corners.

Directions:

1. The coach (C) tosses the ball to put it into play on either side of the net.

2. Two back-court defensive players (X) and a setter (S) at the net are positioned as shown in the diagram. Two additional players are waiting off the court. Every player will play every position.

3. The ball is directed to the setter (S), who sets a back-court attack to the left-back defensive player, who must attack the right back corner of the opponent's court. The ball is received and passed to S, who repeats the action on the other side.

4. After playing the ball, each player moves one position in a clockwise manner, with the extra player moving onto the court.

5. After a period of time, switch the direction of the ball movement to counterclockwise (i.e., the setter sets to a right-back defensive player, who directs the ball to the left back area of the opponent's court).

6. Time the drill for three to five minutes in each direction.

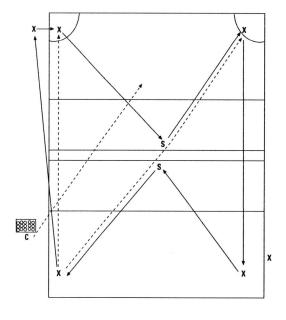

DRILL #47: "CALL FOR THE BALL" ATTACK

Number of Players: 12

Number of Balls: 6

Objective: To promote communication within the team while concentrating on a strong offense and effective transition.

Directions:

1. Set up three lines of hitters (H) vs. three blockers (B).

2. The coach (C) receives balls from the toss line. Whichever hitter (H) communicates will receive a tossed ball. Other offensive players (X) cover while blockers block.

3. The offense makes a quick transition and again communicates to C. H retrieves the ball and goes to the end of the tosser line.

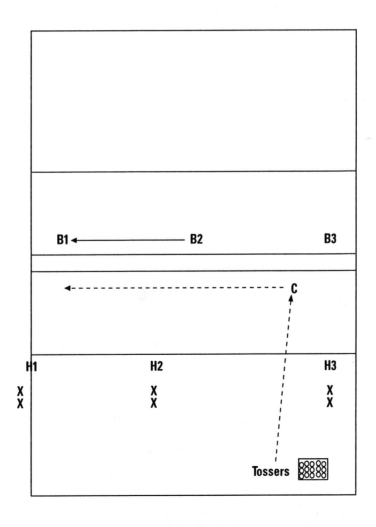

DRILL #48: DETERMINATION AND STAMINA

Number of Players: 3

Number of Balls: 15–20

Objective: To encourage determination and develop stamina in players.

Directions:

1. One coach (C1) tosses the ball short at the 3-meter line.

2. X plays the ball up with a recovery skill.

3. X runs under the net and assumes the left-back defensive position.

4. C2 hits at X.

5. X digs the ball to the target (T).

6. C1 tosses a long ball out of reach of X.

7. X must play the ball up, assuming this is the second ball played on his/her side of the net.

8. Another player begins as soon as X goes for the deep ball.

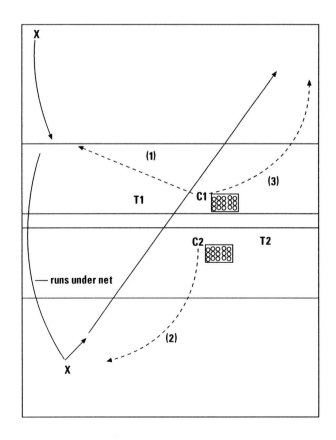

DRILL #49: FREE BALL PASS, QUICK HITTING
AND OUTSIDE HITTING IN TRANSITION

Number of Players: 12–15

Number of Balls: 20–30

Objective: To provide structured opportunities to hit a first-tempo set, followed immediately by an outside, higher set (16).

Directions:

1. Begin the drill with two receiving lines (P), two setters (S), two tossers and two hitters (H).

2. Balls are tossed to passers (P1, P2) in the receiving line who pass the ball to S. Coaches should stress receiving with the overhand pass for passers.

3. Hitter 1 (H1) and Hitter 2 (H2) hit two times consecutively. The first set is quick; the second set is high and outside. Coaches should stress good movement off the net and a good approach for the hitters.

4. Tossers must toss the second ball immediately after the hitters land from the first attack.

5. Passers become hitters; hitters retrieve two balls.

6. Tossers switch into receiving lines after 10 tosses.

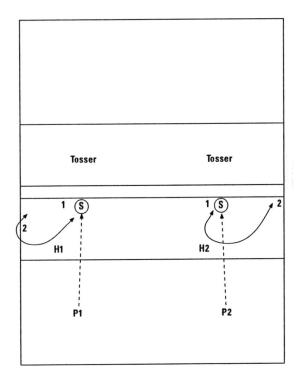

DRILL #50: READ THE BLOCK

Number of Players: 4 or more

Number of Balls: 5 or more

Objective: Players are asked to attack repeatedly against a constantly changing block. This allows the attacker to focus completely on the configuration of the block and learn to adjust the attack.

Directions:

1. The hitter (H) repeatedly attacks five times in a row. Against the attacker are three blockers (B) who decide in which sequence they will block the attacker (i.e., one, all or any combination).

Variations:

1. The drill can be run with only the attack and block, or other variations can be added (e.g., diggers passing to target).

2. The ball can be tossed to the setter or passed by a back-row player to the setter.

3. The attacker can dig to the setter before attacking.

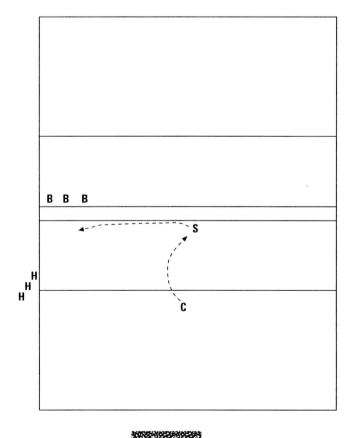

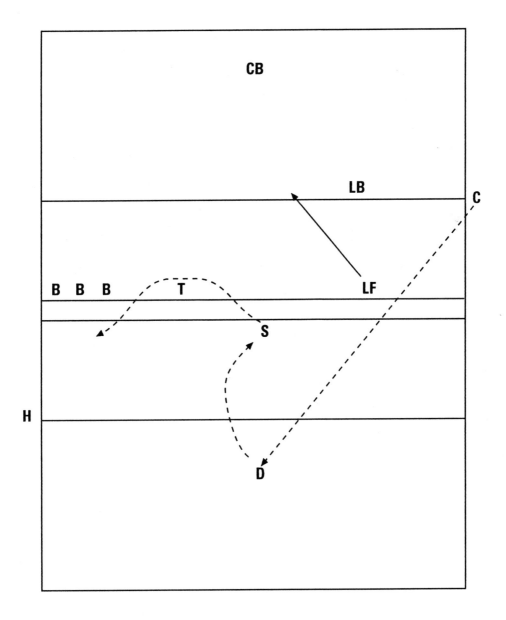

DRILL #51: REPETITION HITTING

Number of Players: 1

Number of Balls: 12 or more

Objective: To give an attacker repeated opportunities to attack, step back and attack again.

Directions:

1. The coach (C) stands next to the hitter (H) and tosses the ball.

2. H must spike the ball, recover and immediately spike the next tossed ball. Complete 10–12 repetitions.

Variations:

1. Have H transition to middle block between each attack.

2. Put a double block against H.

3. Have no block, but have two or three players (D1, D2, D3) play defense.

4. Have C call the zone for the attack as H approaches.

ZONE HITTING VARIATION

H C

(Call zones for attackers during approach)

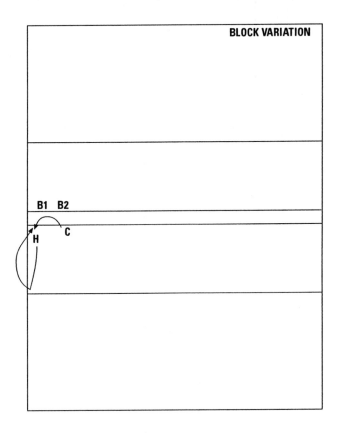

BLOCK VARIATION

B1 B2

C

H

DIGGER VARIATION

D1   D2

D3

C

H

DRILL #52: SHORT BALL + ATTACK

Number of Players: 6–14

Number of Balls: Steady supply

Objective: To work on passing the short, free ball or roll shot and then to work on setting up the attack. The drill works specifically on the transition attack off the short ball passed by the right-front, middle-front and/or left-front hitters.

Directions:

1. The hitter (H1) starts at the net. The coach (C) tosses a short free ball or a short roll shot. H1 transitions back to pass the ball to the setter (S), then sets up for the attack. (Use two setters and two lines of attackers on opposite sides of the net, if necessary.)

2. Alternate free balls or roll shots, with one player on one side going first. Then have the opposite player go next. Keep the drill moving.

3. H1 begins on the left side. The drill then runs the same as above.

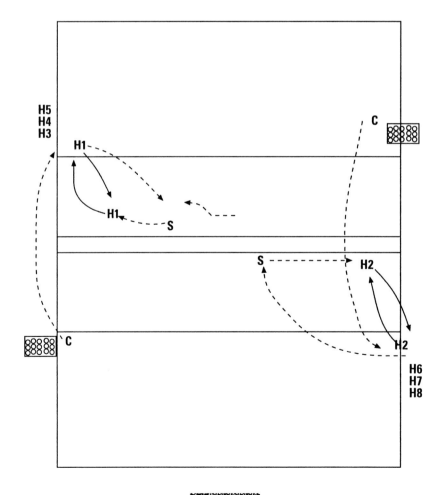

CHAPTER 6

SETTING DRILLS

DRILL #53: 6342 SETTING

Number of Players: 6–12

Number of Balls: 2–4

Objective: To develop setting skills for all members of a team.

Directions:

1.   Start players (P) in positions 6, 3, 4 and 2.

2.   Set the ball from 6 to 3 to 4 to 2 and back to the 6 position. Players must move quickly each time they set the ball to the new position.

Variations:

1.   After the players develop the drill, use two balls in a row.

2.   Start the drill from the 1 or 5 position.

3.   Use six players on each side of the court.

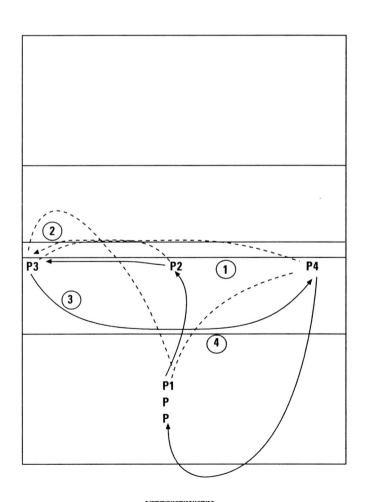

P3   **P2**   **P4**

P1
P
P

Start on 5

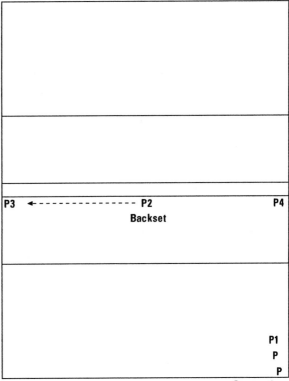

P3 ← - - - - - - - - - - - - - - **P2**   **P4**
Backset

P1
P
P

Start on 1

DRILL #54: BASIC SETTER PRESSURE

Number of Players: 12

Number of Balls: Steady supply

Objective: To give the setter an opportunity to define court presence under high-pressure, game-like situations.

Directions:

1. The setter (S) goes to the setting position; the balls are in the ball cart in position 6 (center back).

2. The hitters (X) form hitting lines. The coach (C) places the hitters in a numerical order. Spread the hitters randomly so that they approach their set from a variety of positions while remaining in the assigned numerical order. C will give S tosses as quickly as possible, while S distributes the sets according to numerical order. Each hitter should call out his/her sequential number at the beginning to assist S in the learning process. As the drill progresses, S should have the sequence memorized and set accordingly.

3. S takes it from there. During the drill, tosses may vary in quality and pace, therein stressing the setter as C deems appropriate. S is practicing leadership, decision making and match management under stress. The goal of this drill is for the hitters to score a consecutive number of kills as determined by C.

4. Explain the parameters of the drill for S. Give the goal and let the setter do the drill. He/she is going to get frazzled, frustrated and may have trouble getting out of the drill. That does not have to be a negative thing! Coach the setter privately and let him/her know that court presence is being developed under these conditions, just as much as the ability to deliver a nice set. If the drill does not become stressful, it is not indicative of the conditions of the match at times.

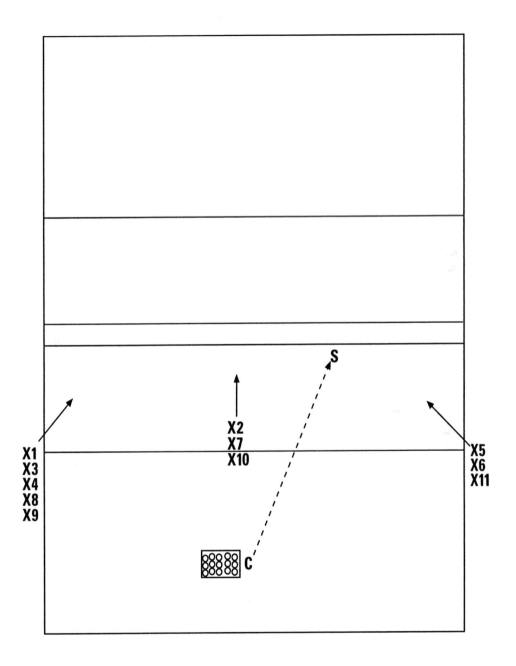

DRILL #55: FOUR-ON-THREE SETTER TRANSITION

Number of Players: 8–12

Number of Balls: 3 or more

Objective: To teach setters and others the importance of transition and the ability to work well together.

Directions:

1. The coach (C) hits a down ball to Team A to initiate the drill. The server (S) must also start on this side.

2. Team A must transition into offense, and Team B must play defense with no block.

3. As soon as team A hits to Team B, S must step under the net and run the offense for Team B.

4. Once the rally has ended, players rotate one position, with players from the sideline rotating into the drill.

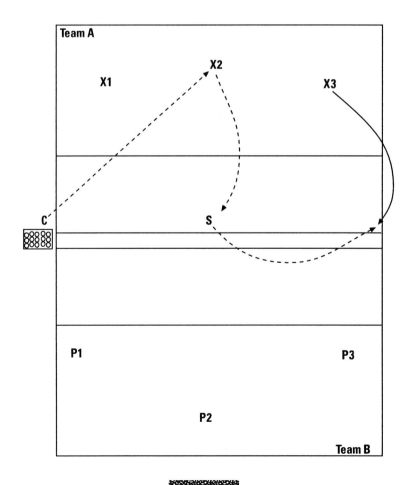

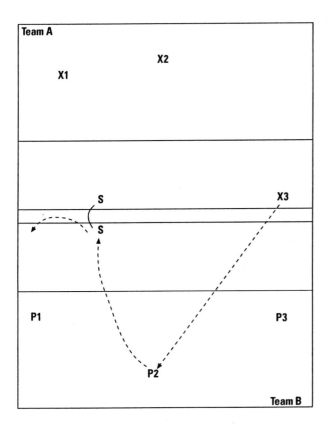

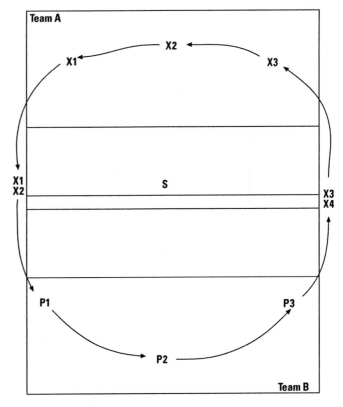

DRILL #56: SETTER MOVEMENT

Number of Players: 1

Number of Balls: 2

Objective: To hasten setter movement to the ball.

Directions:

1. The setter (S) moves as quickly as possible to the target (T) from three serve receive patterns.

2. The coach (C) times the movement and records the times. C adds a toss.

3. Next, S moves as quickly as possible to T through cones, which can be arranged in any fashion. C times the movement and records it. C then adds a toss.

4. S moves quickly to the T. C bounces the ball, and S moves to the ball and sets either left or right side.

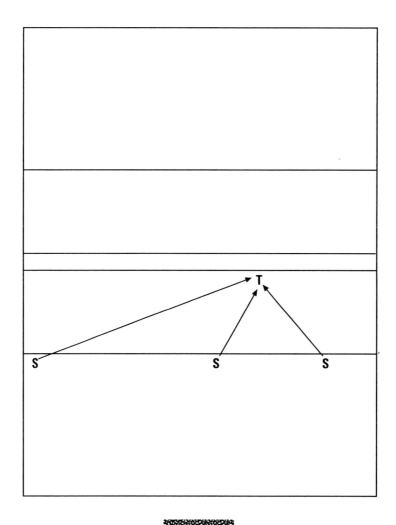

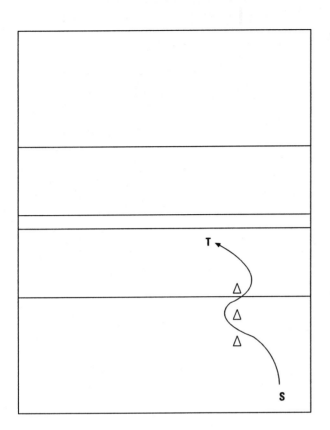

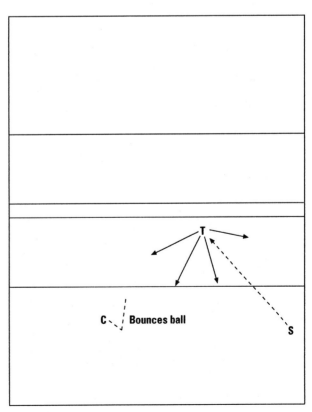

C ⌐ Bounces ball

DRILL #57: SETTER READ

Number of Players: 7

Number of Balls: 6

Objective: To provide opportunities for the setter to "read" the block and set toward gaps.

Directions:

1. Set up three blockers (B1, B2, and B3) on defense.

2. They block left, right or triple middle.

3. The coach (C) starts the drill with a toss to the setter (S).

3. S reads the blockers and sets where they are not.

4. The drill emphasizes the use of peripheral vision by the setter in order to make appropriate setting decisions for the hitters (H1, H2 and H3).

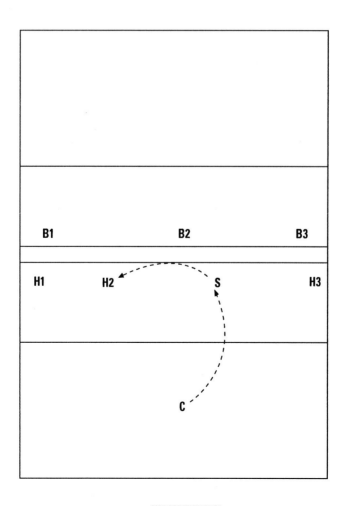

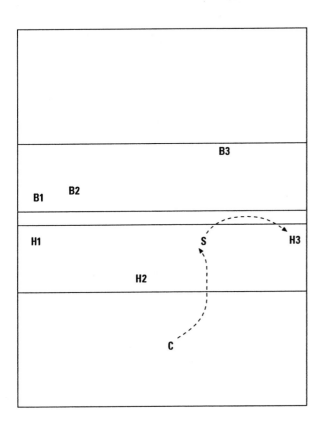

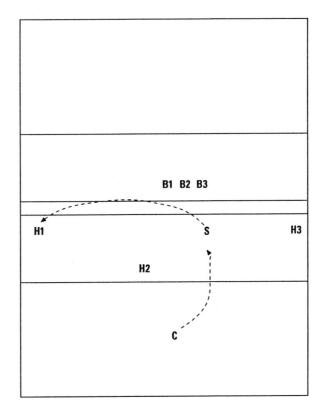

DRILL #58: CUSTER'S LAST STAND

Number of Players: 9–12

Number of Balls: 1

Objective: This drill encourages team unity while keeping the players on their toes. No one knows to whom the setter is going to set and the players never know whom the coach is going to send into the middle.

Directions:

1. The setter (S) begins by setting any player (P) on the circle. That player then downballs to the middle of the circle to one of the diggers (D), who passes to the setter.

2. The cycle continues. When a digger makes an error, that player is replaced by someone from the circle until everybody has been "killed."

Variations:

1. Have S call out the name of the player who will receive the set.

2. Use only one digger.

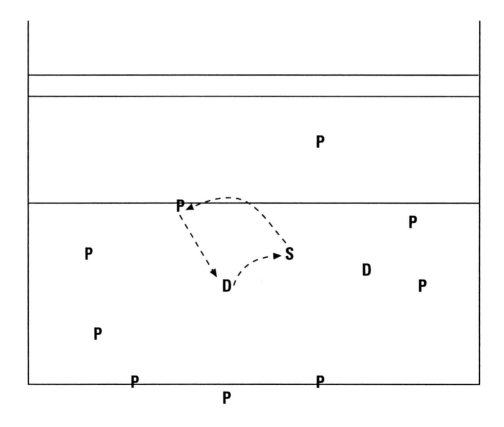

CHAPTER 7

TRANSITION DRILLS

DRILL #59: 4 ON 4 X 4 = 4 + 4

Number of Players: 12 or more

Number of Balls: Steady supply

Objective: This drill is a more specific version of the "King/Queen of the Court" drill, which all players love. This drill is competitive, develops ball control, forces players to concentrate on one contact at a time and requires them to move quickly from different points on the court between contacts.

Directions:

1. The drill is run with a winner's side and a challenger's side (with the coach [C] and the losing team retrieving the ball). C starts the rally with a serve.

2. The setters (S1 and S2) can set, block, dump or attack overpasses/overdigs.

3. Defenders (P) (on C's side) must start with a foot on the 3-meter line. They cannot move from that spot until S1 sets or dumps. If S1 dumps, defenders react to play the ball.

4. If S1 sets, then defenders must back up quickly and position themselves behind the blocker, still balanced and ready for the attack. Attackers must hit from behind the 3-meter line. The blocker should block on every attempt possible (which forces the attacker's teammates to watch the block and cover).

5. Once the ball enters the opponent's side of the court, the blocker assumes the ready position at the net, and the back-court players hustle to the 3-meter line to be ready for the opposing setter to handle the ball.

6. Continue as long as the rally lasts. The loser retrieves the balls and returns to C's side to await his/her turn. The winner stays or crosses over to the side opposite C to receive serve.

7. Four wins in a row means four sit-ups and push-ups for everyone else.

Winner's Side

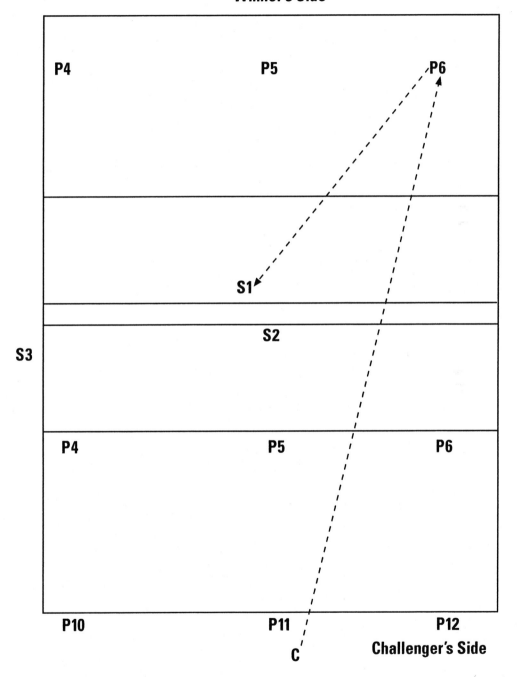

DRILL #60: ATTACK, DIG, ATTACK, BLOCK, DIG

Number of Players: Unlimited

Number of Balls: 12 or more

Objective: This is a high-intensity drill where the attacker attacks, digs, quick attacks, blocks, turns and digs.

Directions:

1. One hitter (X1) attacks the ball tossed by a coach (C1) in the left front. X2 waits until he/she is ready to go.

2. X1 transitions off the net, digging a down ball from C4.

3. After the dig, X1 comes in for a quick attack off a toss from C2.

4. After attacking, X1 moves to the right front and blocks an attack from C3.

5. Immediately after blocking, X1 turns and digs the ball from C4.

6. X2 begins the drill in attack phase after X1's block lands on the floor.

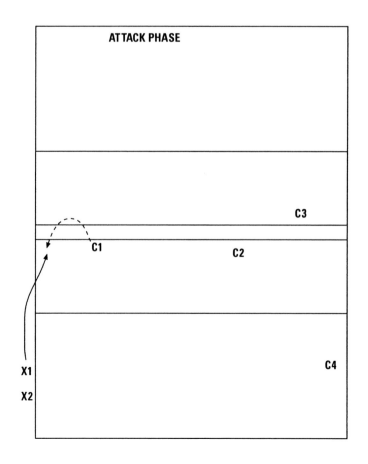

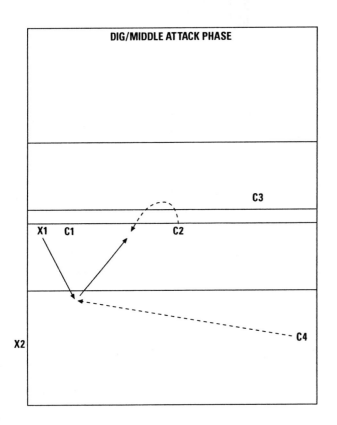

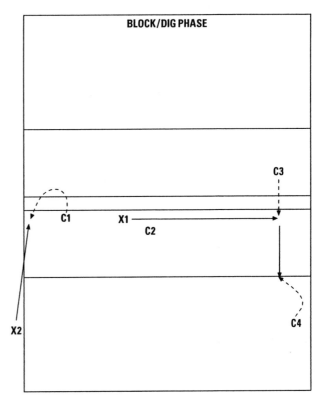

DRILL #61: 5-ON-5

Number of Players: 10

Number of Balls: 1

Objective: This drill is used to teach back-court defense when the block is not closed out and to teach outside blockers the importance of proper hand movement, as well as to concentrate on the ball as they solo block.

Directions:

1. Set up two teams (X, P) with five players each. The middle blocker at the net is absent.

2. The coach (C) "frees" a ball onto either side of the court, and the point is played out.

3. Repeat the drill several times and then rotate.

4. If the setter (S) is in the back row, set the outside hitter or the right-side hitter. If S is at the net, set the outside hitter or the right back (D-set) or the middle back (pipe).

5. Teams play their normal defense and work on adjusting to this new situation.

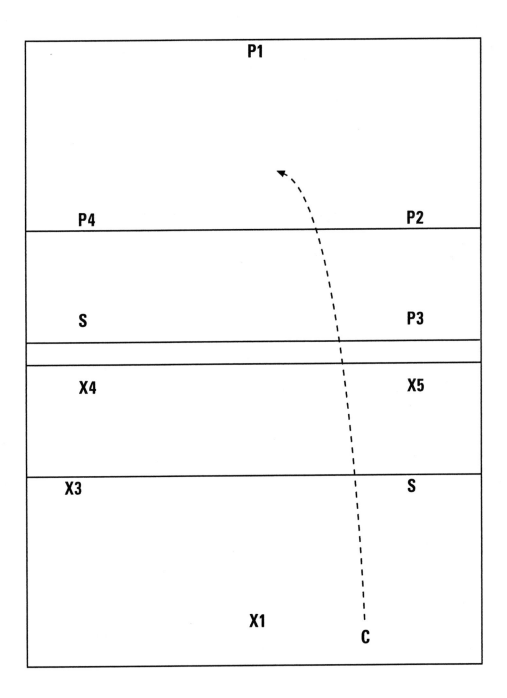

DRILL #62: BLOCK/TRANSITION ATTACK

Number of Players: 8–15

Number of Balls: 12

Objective: This drill was developed to work on middle hitter blocking fundamentals and transition footwork to attack.

Directions:

1. The coach (C) is on one side of the net in the back row with a ball cart and the setter (S), right front (RF) and middle hitter (MH). On the opposite side of the net is a middle blocker (MB), S and a line of hitters (H).

2. C freeballs over the net to H1, who passes the ball to S and then transitions outside to attack power. On C's side of the net, RF and MF close to form a block.

3. Immediately after the attack, whether the ball is blocked or not, S penetrates and C tosses a second ball to him/her. As this is occurring, both the right-side and middle blockers transition off the net and enter into their attack patterns. Any attack may be used, including playsets. As they mount their attack, the opposing middle and outside hitters prepare to block. Once the second ball goes down, the entire procedure is repeated again, with C sending a free ball over to H2.

Scoring:

1. The drill can be scored for points. Typically, one stuff block, followed immediately by a successful kill, equals one point. It is scored in wash fashion. If a stuff block is followed by an unsuccessful kill attempt, then no point is scored. Play to 10 points.

Variation:

1. On C's side, have a front-row S with MH and a power hitter. In this scenario, the opposite side has S and a line of right-side hitters. The first ball is sent to the first right-side hitter in line on the other side of the net who passes, transitions outside and attacks. On C's side, the MH and power hitter form a block. Then, immediately after the block, regardless of the result, C tosses the second ball to S, who sets either the middle or the power hitter vs. the opposing right-side and middle blockers.

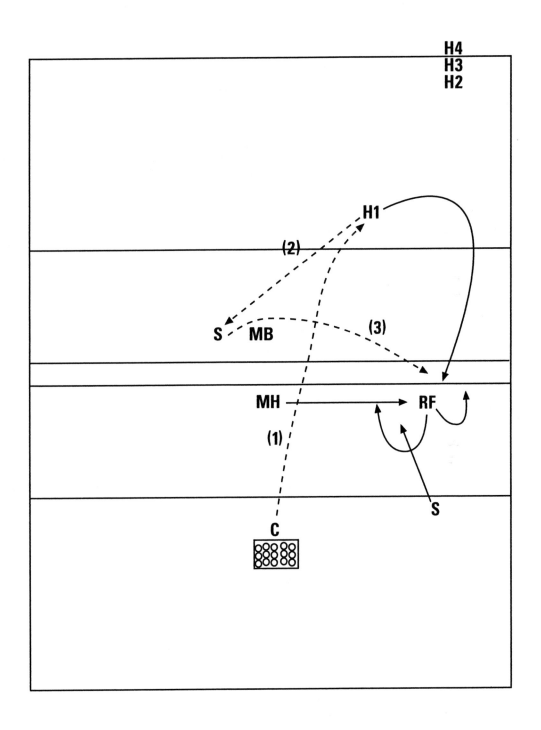

DRILL #63: CONTINUOUS TRANSITION

Number of Players: 12

Number of Balls: 12

Objective: To provide opportunities to pass a down ball to target and work on free ball combination offense.

Directions:

1. One coach (C1) hits the down ball to the digger (D1).

2. D1 digs and one setter (S1) sets any of the three hitters (LH, MH, RH).

3. After the ball is terminated, C2 hits the down ball at D2, who digs, and S2 sets any of the three hitters.

4. Repeat.

Variations:

1. Free Ball Play No. 1 involves the middle hitter hitting a 31 and the right-side hitter hitting either a 52 or a 51.

2. Free Ball Play No. 2 involves the same as No. 1, except D2 hits a back-row set.

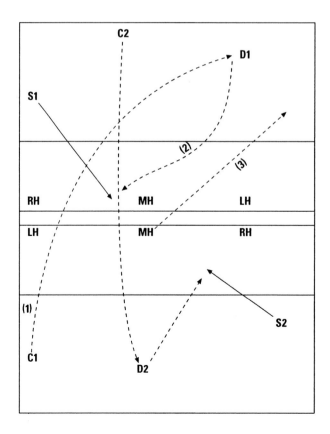

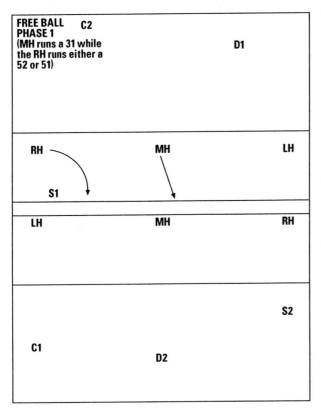

FREE BALL
PHASE 1
(MH runs a 31 while
the RH runs either a
52 or 51)

C2

D1

RH   MH   LH

S1

LH   MH   RH

S2

C1

D2

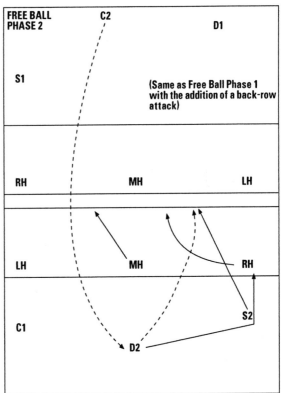

FREE BALL
PHASE 2

C2

D1

S1

(Same as Free Ball Phase 1
with the addition of a back-row
attack)

RH   MH   LH

LH   MH   RH

S2

C1

D2

DRILL #64: CROSS-COURT DIG/SET/ATTACK

Number of Players: 6 or more

Number of Balls: Steady supply

Objective: This drill incorporates decreased court size and changing orientation to the court to encourage improved ballhandling and to help players become savvy; the drill concentrates on ball handling and warm-up/conditioning.

Directions:

1. The coach (C) puts the ball in play by tossing or hitting to players on either side of the net.

2. Players pass, set, hit to athletes on the other side of the net. To be successful, the ball must land in the cross-court half of the opposing court.

3. Players rotate each time they put the ball across the net successfully. When more than three players on a side are involved, a line is formed with players rotating in and out as play continues.

Variations:

1. For inexperienced players: the game is played competitively with both sides working together to accomplish a certain number of continuous, successful volleys.

2. For intermediate players: the game is played cooperatively until a number of successful volleys are reached; then, without stopping, the game is played competitively with setters and blockers. (Setters are not required to remain within court boundaries.)

3. For advanced players: go for it!

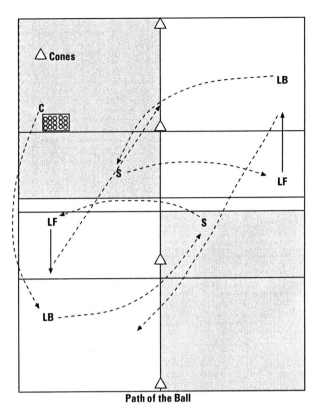

Path of the Ball

Rotation of Players

DRILL #65: FIVE VS. FIVE

Number of Players: 10

Number of Balls: Steady supply

Objective: To enhance the blocker's ability to read the hitter's approach and take away the hitter's angle. Blockers will block one-on-one and they must read the hitter and the block accordingly. The defenders should position themselves around the block.

Directions:

1. Teams are divided on opposite sides of the net, occupying each position except middle front.

2. Down balls from the coach (C) initiate play. Alternate sides that receive the down ball to create wash scoring.

3. The setter (S), who plays right back, can set all available hitters.

4. One team must win both rallies to earn a point. If the teams split rallies, a wash occurs and the process is repeated.

5. Each game is played to +3, with the winning team staying on the court.

Variations:

1. Vary the initiated ball to allow for more or less control, depending on the players' skill level.

2. Serve the initiated ball to emphasize passing.

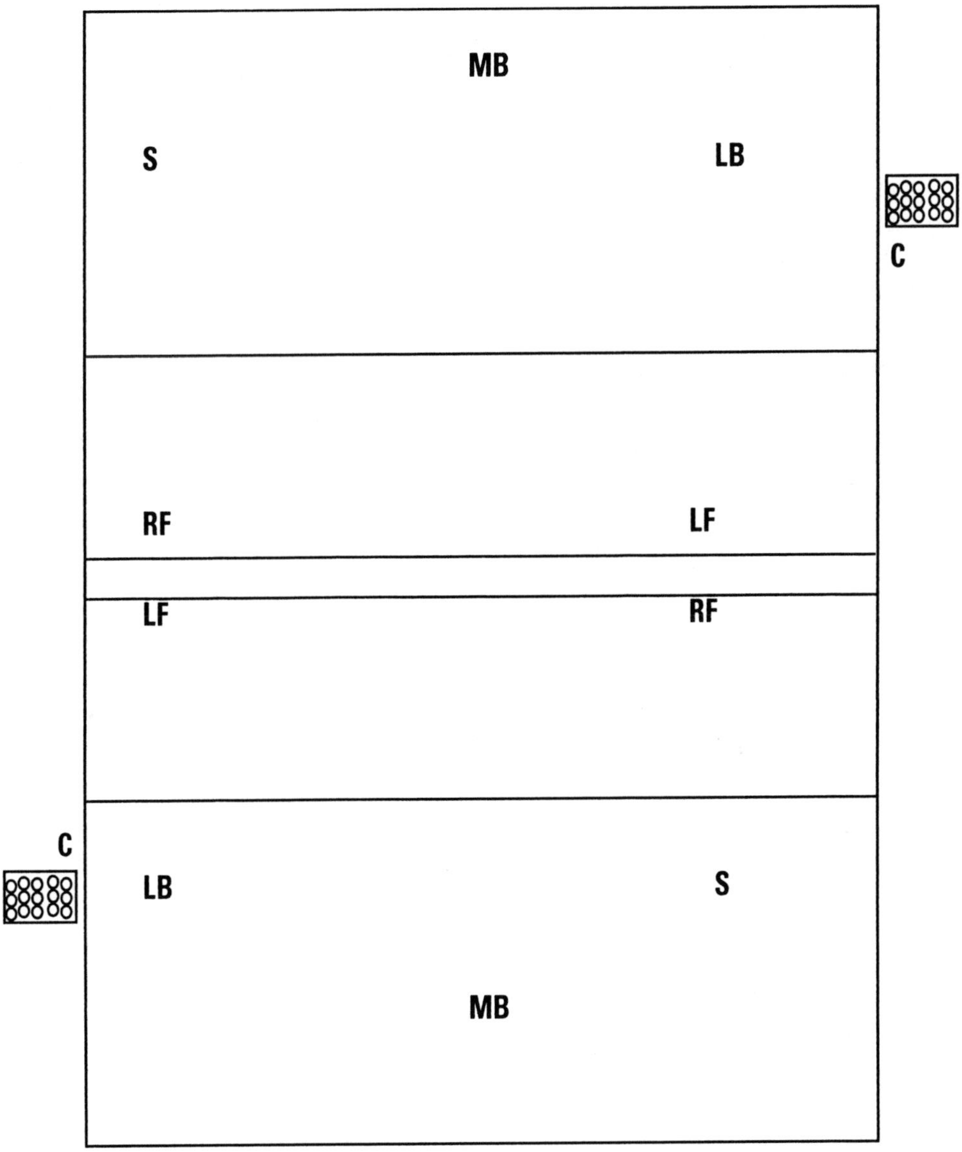

MB

S   LB

                          ⬚ C

RF   LF

LF   RF

C ⬚

LB   S

MB

DRILL #66: DEEP HIT KING/QUEEN OF THE NARROW COURT

Number of Players: 8–10

Number of Balls: 1

Objective: To practice all skills, including deep hitting.

Directions:

1. Two players set up on the receiving side of the net, while the rest of the team (six to eight players) sets up in lines on the serving side of a 15' x 30' court.

2. The teams go two against two. Play until a rally is won.

3. If the receivers win, they record a point and stay. If the servers win, they advance to the receiving (scoring) side.

4. Two new players come in each time to the serving side of the net. Keep the drill running quickly so that players are always on their toes.

4. The first team to win five consecutive points on the receiving side wins. All non-winners will do 10 tuck jumps, while the winners will do five.

5. Two narrow court games can be played concurrently.

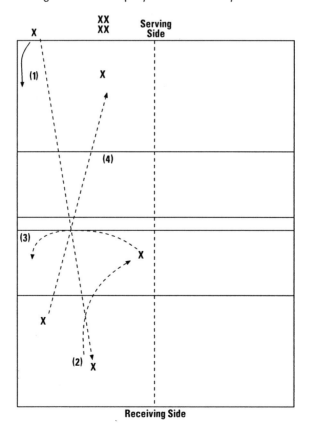

DRILL #67: FOUR-ON-FOUR FRONTLINE WASH

Number of Players: 8–10

Number of Balls: Steady supply

Objective: To improve free ball and transition movement and playset execution with a strong block in competitive situations.

Directions:

1. The coach (C) on Side B initiates a free ball to Side A.

2. Team A releases from the net to free ball position with setter (S) penetration.

3. Team A runs the designated playset while Team B reads and blocks.

4. Continue the rally until terminated.

5. If Team A wins the rally, it gets one point. If Team B wins the rally, it is a wash. Whoever wins the rally gets the next free ball and a chance to score.

6. Play to a designated point total.

Variations:

1. After designated points are reached, switch attackers or middle blockers.

2. Give a point for a stuff block.

3. Add a digger/ passer to the back row.

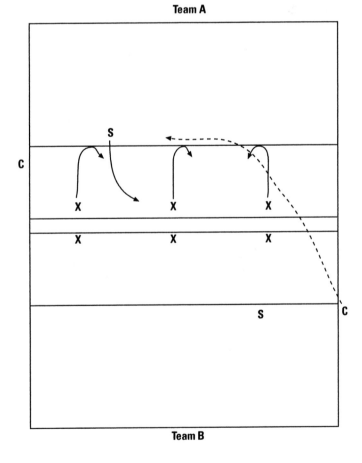

4. Allow a team to score only on a particular playset (31, 51, slide, etc.).

DRILL #68: FOUR-ON-FOUR HITTERS VS. DIGGERS

Number of Players: Multiples of 4

Number of Balls: Steady supply

Objective: To provide transition opportunities in a competitive situation, hitting from a minimum of 5 feet from the net, allowing more digs to occur.

Directions:

1. Divide the players into groups of four, with each group having fairly equal ability.

2. One group of four becomes the diggers and blocker.

3. Everyone else is on the opposite side of the net and is eligible to attack after digging an attack by the coach (C).

4. All hitters must go up in front of and come down behind a 5-foot restraining line.

5. The game is three points rally scoring.

6. The loser goes off and a new team comes on.

7. The teams must rotate one position after every point won.

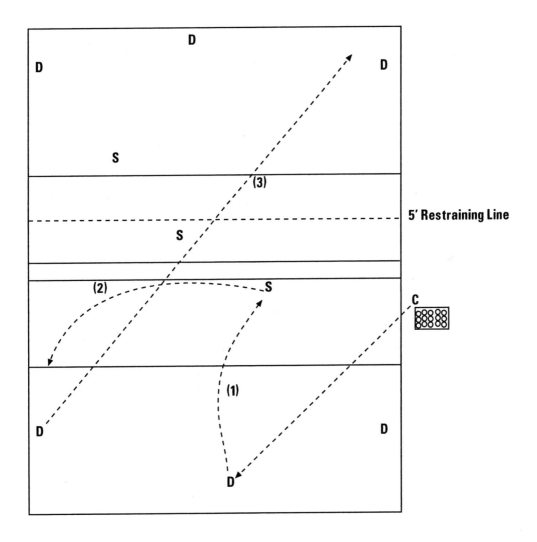

5' Restraining Line

DRILL #69: FRONT COURT TRANSITION

Number of Players: 8

Number of Balls: Steady supply

Objective: This is a high repetition drill for practicing transition, setting, attacking and blocking.

Directions:

1. The coach (C) initiates the drill by slapping the ball. At contact, one setter (S2) penetrates and sets to any of the three hitters.

2. The offensive side keeps transitioning until it gets a kill. If blocked, C2 tosses another ball.

3. After getting a kill, LH2, MH2 and RH2 become blockers, and the other side of the net becomes the offense.

4. Play continues until a designated number of kills or blocks has been reached.

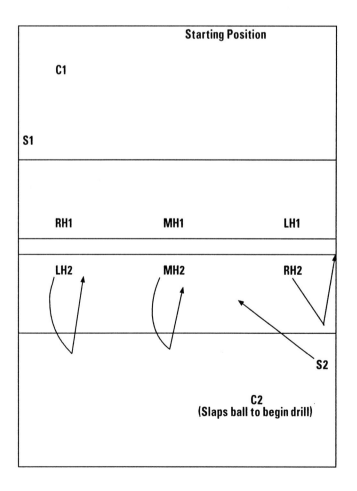

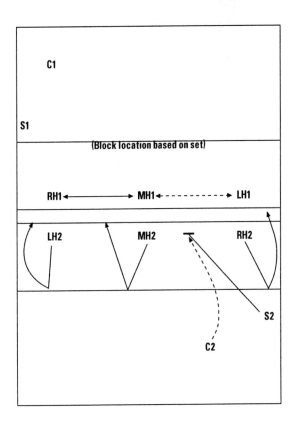

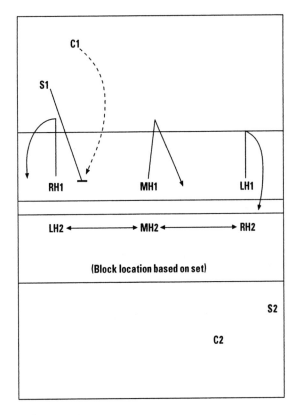

DRILL #70: M+M

Number of Players: 8

Number of Balls: 8–12

Objective: To train middle blockers to attack and block alternately at a rapid pace.

Directions:

1. The coach (C) gives a free or down ball to one side, which must set the middle blocker (MB1).

2. MB2 commits and tries to stop the attack.

3. If there is a stuff block or the hitter makes an error, MB2 leads, 1-0.

4. C changes sides of the net and gives a free or down ball to Side 2.

5. If MB2 sides out, the score is still M2 = 1, M1 = 0.

6. C changes sides every time.

7. A point is scored with the stuff block or an opponent error. The first one to three points wins. The loser stays and the winner is replaced.

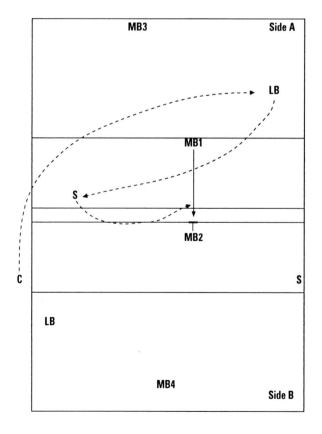

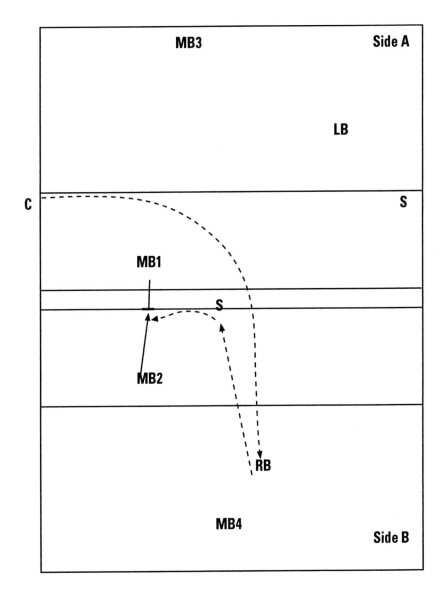

DRILL #71: NO BOUNDARIES

Number of Players: 4–12

Number of Balls: Steady supply

Objective: This is a defensive team drill that teaches players to have no mental barriers—just go for the ball. It eliminates the decision process – *if* a player should play the ball. During the drill, it is emphasized that relentless efforts should be made for every ball that crosses the net.

Directions:

1. Equal teams are set up in defensive positions. The cooperative drill is actually a pepper game where players on both sides of the net are working together to keep the ball in play.

2. There are no court boundaries for the game, only a net. All of the rules of volleyball pertain to the drill, except there is no such thing as an "out" ball. Every ball that crosses the net is playable.

3. If a rally should end, the coach (C) initiates play by creating the same scenario that caused the rally to end.

Goals:

1. The goals for the drill can include having the ball cross the net 10 times or keeping the ball in play for one minute. The drill becomes fun for the players as their defensive attitudes develop.

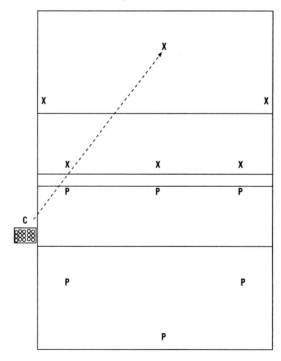

DRILL #72: PEPPER OVER THE NET

Number of Players: 9 (3 per group)

Number of Balls: 1 per group

Objective: To promote line hitting with continuous ball control.

Directions:

1. Set up three players with one ball on one side of the court. The setter (S) sets to the hitter (e.g., LS, M, RS) at 7 to 8 feet from the net.

2. The hitter takes off as a back-row hitter and hits to the adjacent digger.

3. The digger digs the ball to S at the net, who sets again to the hitter.

Variation:

1. Use a standing topspin hit.

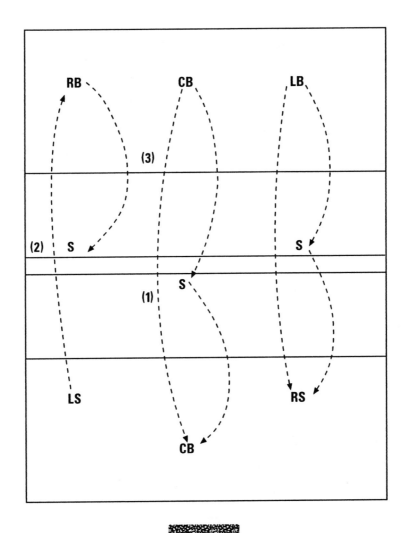

DIAGRAM #73: QUICK HITTING TRANSITION

Number of Players: 10

Number of Balls: 24

Objective: To encourage transition involving quick middle and back-row attacking.

Directions:

1. The drill requires two teams of five players each: one setter (S), one quick hitter/middle blocker (QH); three back-row hitters/diggers (LB, CB, RB). Also, make sure there are two ball retrievers, one coach (C) and one scorer.

2. C starts the drill by hitting a ball at Team A.

3. Team A attempts to pass the ball to the setter well enough to run a quick attack. (The only allowed attacks at the net are quick hits.)

4. If the ball is set to the back-row players, they must attack behind the 3-meter line.

5. As soon as the ball is dead, C hits a ball at Team B, and the players attempt a quick transition.

6. If both teams score one each, it is a wash. If one of the teams scores both 1/2 points, it scores a point.

7. C can make the first hits hard or easy, according to the players' ability.

8. At four or five points, rotate the QH.

9. Keep the balls playable when hitting to begin each series.

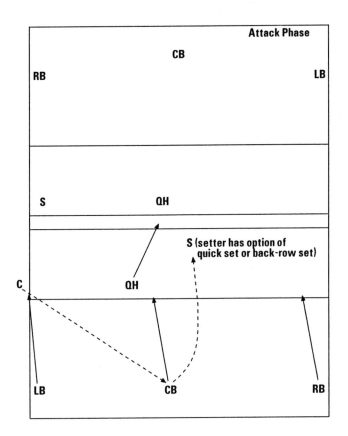

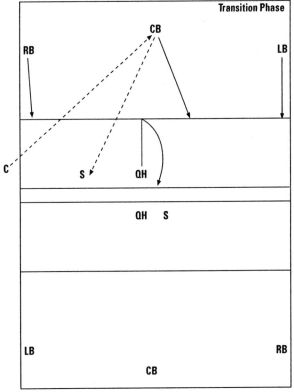

DRILL #74: THREE VS. SIX SIDE OUT OR SIDE OFF

Number of Players: 9–15

Number of Balls: 4–6

Objective: To provide a good, fast, game-like workout where every point counts, forcing players of unequal skill to work together (six against three).

Directions:

1. Set up three teams or more of three players each. Put Team No. 1 (X1) on one side of the net, with Team No. 2 (X2) on the opposite side, front row. Team No. 3 (X3) goes on the opposite side in the back row. If there is a Team No. 4 (X4), put it in the challenger's back line. Team No. 5 retrieves the balls and then takes Team No. 4's place.

2. The coach (C) sends a free ball to Team No. 1's side, which attacks the six-player side. If they score, they get one point and receive another free ball. If the side of six wins the point, the players rotate in waves.

3. Team No. 1 takes Team No. 5's place, 5 to 4, 4 to 3, 3 to 2. Team No. 2 is now the receiving team. The game continues until one of the teams has five points.

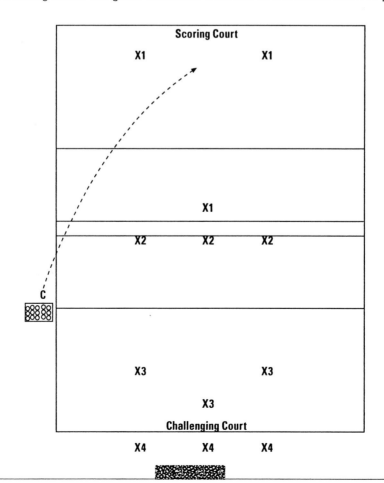

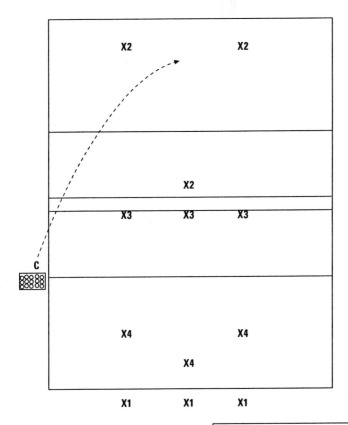

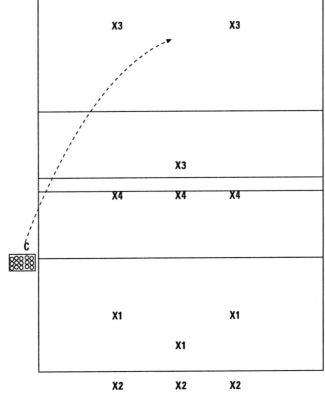

DRILL #75: TRANSITION DEFENSE TO HITTING

Number of Players: 6 or more

Number of Balls: Steady supply

Objective: To provide opportunities to transition from defense to offense.

Directions:

1. The coach (C), standing on a stable platform, attacks the ball to the back-row defender (LB). C can move along the net to attack from various positions.

2. The setter (S) releases to position, while the hitter (H) transitions off the net.

3. LB passes the ball to S.

4. S sets H for the attack.

5. Continue the drill for a specified number of hits.

Variations:

1. Different defenders can be used.

2. Blockers can be added.

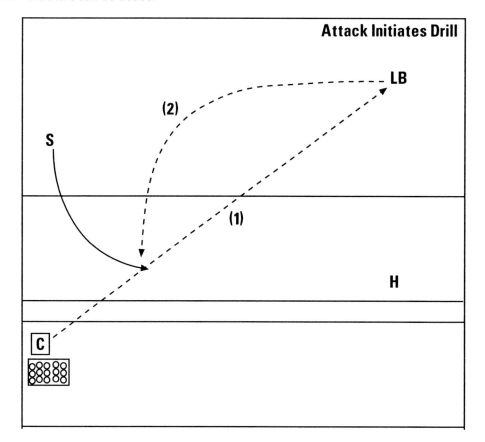

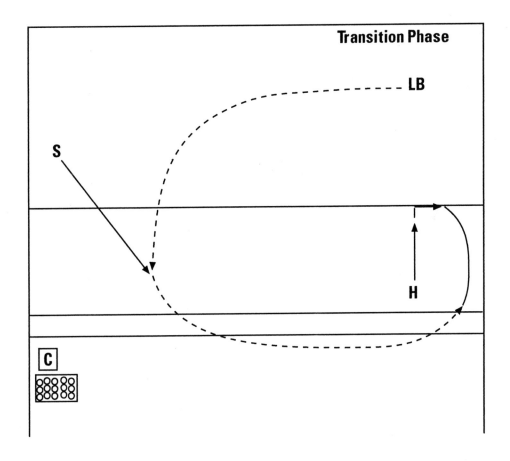

DRILL #76: THREE-ON-FOUR SIDEOUT PRESSURE

Number of Players: 12 or more

Number of Balls: 30 or more

Objective: To side out and put away one transition ball to score.

Directions:

1. One side has three digger-attackers and no designated setter. All other players are in the serving area behind the team of three. The ball must be attacked from behind the 3-meter line on either side.

2. The servers (X) put the ball into play, and if the team of four can pass and put the ball away, it receives a second ball from the coach (C).

3. A point is scored if they can put the second ball away. Only the team of four can score points.

4. Players wave through in groups of three, and the setter always stays. If the team of four puts the first ball away, but not the second, it is a wash and it stays to receive another serve. If they make an error on the first ball, they are off, and a new team of three replaces them.

5. Play games of five to 15, depending on how much time there is to spend on the drill.

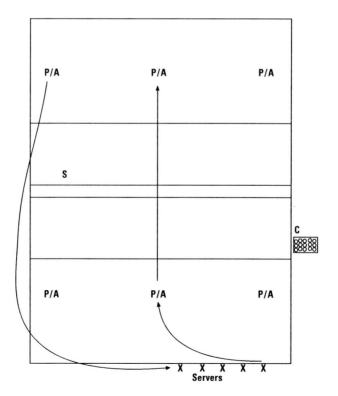

DRILL #77: TRANSITION OFF A TIPPED BALL

Number of Players: 2–3

Number of Balls: Steady supply

Objective: To train the right-front (RF) and right-back (RB) players to coordinate to make good, quick transitions off the opponent's offspeed shots (mainly tips). This is especially helpful if a team runs a rotational defense against a team without great outside hitters.

Directions:

1. The right-front (RF) and center front (CF) players must first block jump. The coach (C) then tips the ball over the block.

2. The right-back player (RB) digs the ball high enough so that RF has time to turn and get under the ball and set to either MF or LF.

Variation:

1. C can replace RB and simulate bad digs by tossing the ball in different areas at different heights and speeds. Challenge RF by varying the tosses. RF will have to find the ball, run it down and still make a good set, either overhand or underhand. Constant repetition will make the RF comfortable in making this play in a match.

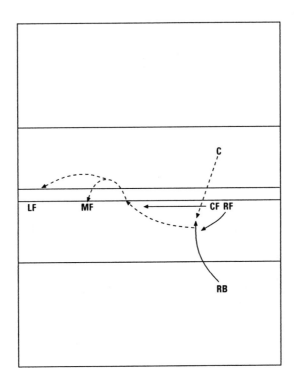

DRILL #78: TWO-ON-THREE TRANSITION

Number of Players: 12

Number of Balls: Steady supply

Objective: To emphasize the importance of putting away the first ball on transition, since continued play favors defense (with three players against the two initially on offense).

Directions:

1. The coach (C) hits a down ball to the passer (P1), who passes to the setter (S1).

2. S1 moves to the setter position and sets an attack ball to P1.

3. The defensive team on the other side (D1, D2, D3) plays the attack. Both sides play the ball until the rally is concluded.

4. S1 and P1 rotate to the end of their respective lines, and S2 and P2 enter the court to continue the drill.

5. After a set limit of rallies, the groups (S, D, P, retrievers) rotate. The drill continues.

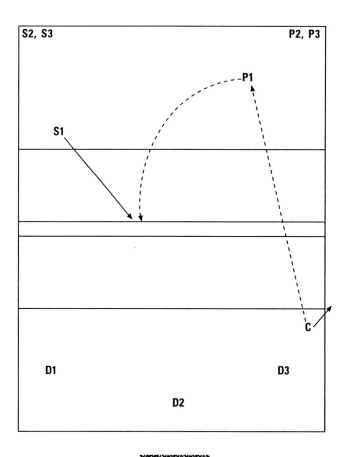

DRILL #79: TWO VS. FOUR TRANSITION OFFENSE

Number of Players: 10–12

Number of Balls: 2 or more

Objective: To stress the necessity of putting the ball down off a good set.

Directions:

1. The coach (C) bounces the ball to the setter (S1), who sets for the hitter (H1).

2. H1 attacks the ball, and the four players on defense (B, D) attempt to play the ball back against S1 and H1—thus a four vs. two.

3. Play continues until one side wins.

4. The winners stay on and the losers are replaced. For example, if S1 and H1 win, they stay on the court and B and the three Ds all leave the court and are replaced by their teammates.

5. After the players are set, C bounces the next ball immediately, keeping the tempo brisk.

6. The drill continues until both hitters lose three times with each setter. Then everyone rotates one spot and resumes play. Play continues until everyone has played all five or six spots. Players not in the drill will retrieve balls until it is their turn on the court.

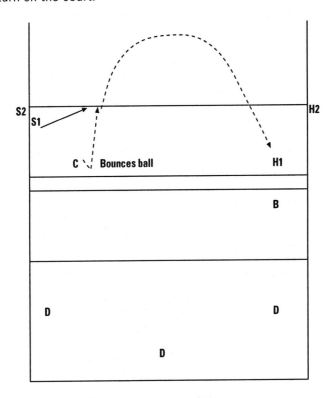

CHAPTER 8

TEAM OFFENSE DRILLS

DRILL #80: 13-0 BLOCKING

Number of Players: 12

Number of Balls: 1

Objective: This drill asks that the team block to score a point; as a result, the drill can be used to teach new blocking schemes, promote better concentration with blocking technique and reward aggressive offense and defense. Blockers realize that taking away the hitter's best swing and forcing the hitter to put more air under the ball results in an advantage for their team.

Directions:

1. Set up a six-on-six drill with the serving team leading, 13-0. (This team will always serve during the drill.)

2. Rally scoring is used. However, the only way the serving team may score is with a stuff block. The receiving team may score any way possible. (The competitive hitters will know if they are never blocked; the serving team cannot score, so the tip may become a weapon.)

4. To offset this conservative approach, the serving team may register a point if it can pick up that tip and convert on the first swing transition.

Variations:

1. Change the starting score (e.g., 12-8).

2. Immediately award a point to the blocking team if a hitter tips.

3. Waive the block requirement for the entire rally, once a ball is tipped or rolled.

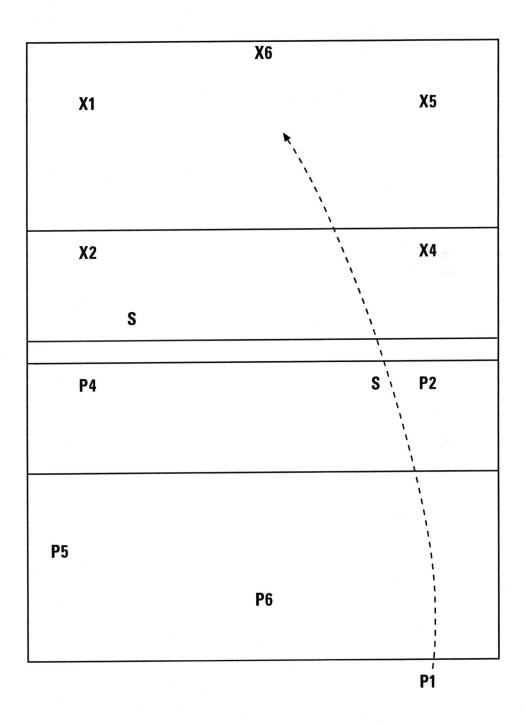

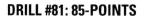

DRILL #81: 85-POINTS

Number of Players: 10

Number of Balls: 10 or more

Objective: To encourage players to pass to the target and attack accurately and consistently while under time constraints.

Directions:

1. Segment 1 (five minutes): The server (X) serves to the passer (P), who passes the ball to the setter (S) on target. Tape the area off as a passing zone. If S receives the ball on or in the taped area, a point is awarded. S sets H1 in area 4. If the attack is good, then a point is awarded. (No tips unless specified.)

2. Segment 2 (five minutes): The same as Segment 1, except the attack is in area 3. Change things up and award two points on a good, quick shoot (31) or slide attack.

3. Segment 3 (five minutes): Same as 1 and 2 with an area 2 attack. Point variations apply.

4. The objective is to collect 85 points.

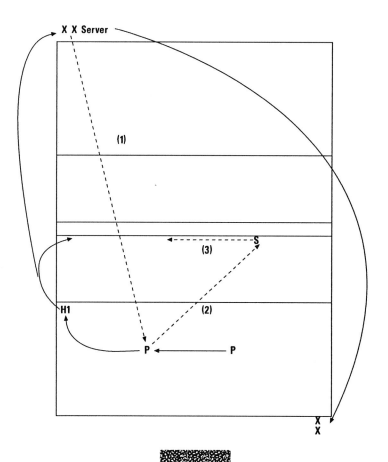

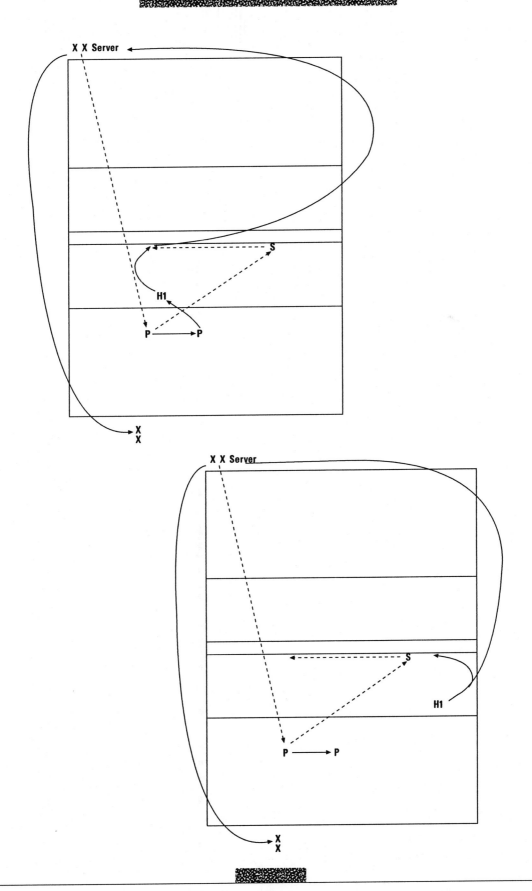

DRILL #82: BONUSBALL

Number of Players: 12

Numbers of Balls: 8 or more

Objective: This drill motivates players to execute, as there is an advantage to being the first team to earn the "bonusball." Players learn that while rallies are important, one needs to practice making "percentage" decisions on crucial plays.

Directions:

1. Two coaches (C1, C2) begin off-court near the 3-meter line. Each coach has three white volleyballs and one colored volleyball—the "bonusball." A basket of extra volleyballs is placed between the coaches.

2. Each team starts in its defensive alignment in the first rotation. Each rally is initiated by a toss or attack from the coach opposite them (ranging from an easy free ball to a difficult down ball.) The winner of each rally wins the next ball.

3. The first team to win three rallies gets its "bonusball." The first team to win six rotations wins the drill. If a team wins a rally on its "bonusball" rally, then play stops and they quickly rotate while their opponent stays in the same rotation. If a team loses its "bonusball" rally, then it receives the balls from the basket on each rally it wins until the opponent earns its "bonusball" and a chance to win a rotation. If neither team wins a "bonusball," then neither team rotates, and the drill begins again.

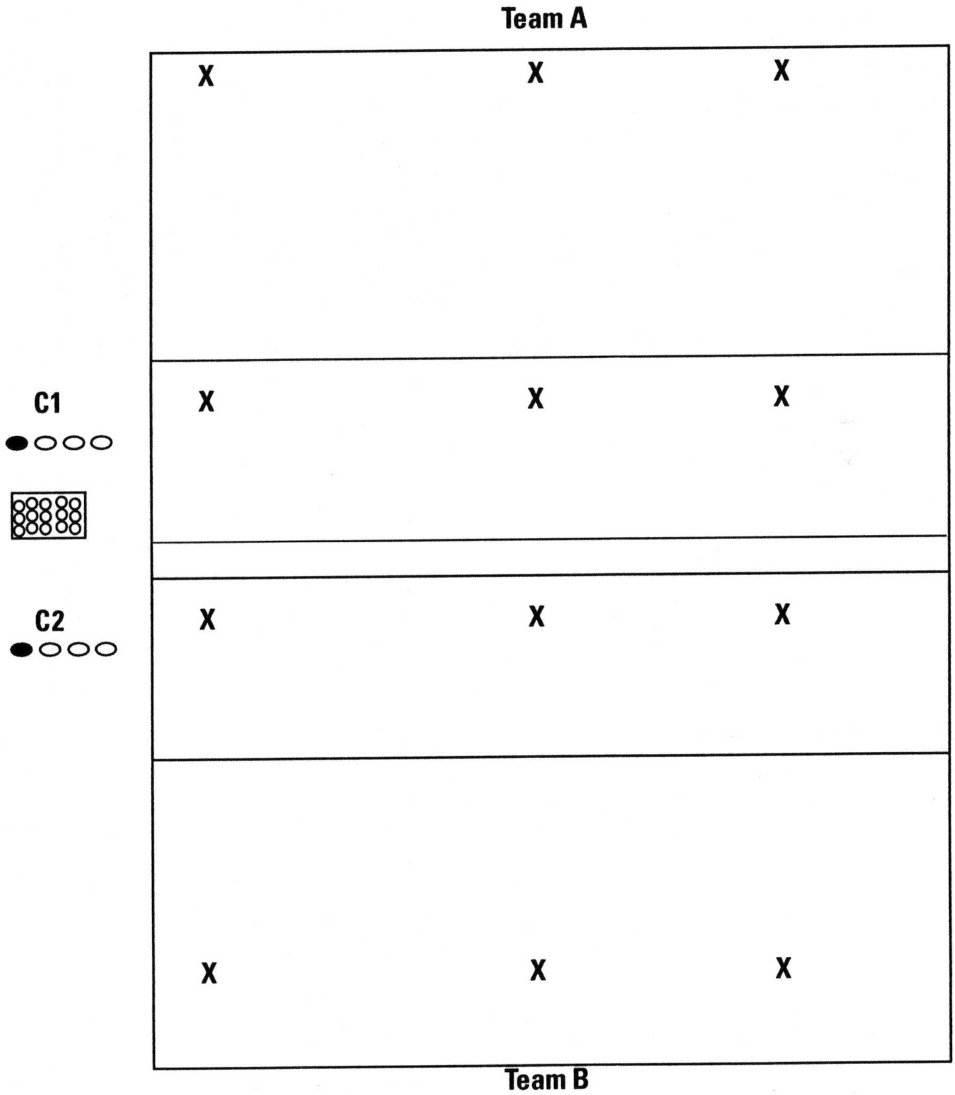

Team A

X	X	X

C1
●○○○

▦

X	X	X

X	X	X

C2
●○○○

X	X	X

Team B

DRILL #83: ROTATION BOOGIE

Number of Players: 12

Number of Balls: Steady supply

Objective: This is a very challenging six-on-six game in which every point counts and the primary focus is on both side-out and free ball offense, as well as serving and transition in defense.

Directions:

1. Set up two teams of six players on opposite sides of the court. Team A sets up to receive a serve, and Team B sets up to serve and play defense.

2. If Team A sides out, it receives four free balls from Coach B. If Team B wins the rally, it sets up to receive serve from Side A and attempts to side out in order also to receive four free balls. After a team receives four free balls, it then serves to the other team.

Scoring:

1. Free ball points are tallied on a visible scoreboard. When one team earns five free ball points, it then receives a "boogie point" and both teams rotate. After six rotations, the team with the most "boogie points" is the winner.

Variations:

1. Change the number of free balls necessary to earn a "boogie point."

2. A team can only score a free ball point on a particular play (e.g., 2-1-9, 5-8-2).

3. Change the coach throwing free balls to the coach hitting down balls.

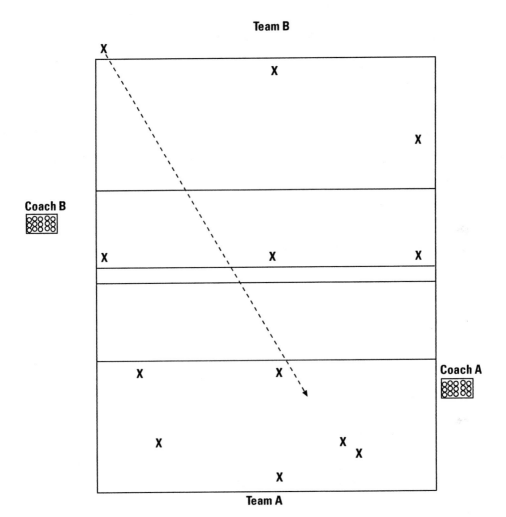

DRILL #84: HUNTS OR "KETCHUP"

Number of Players: 12

Number of Balls: Steady supply

Objective: To help develop pace and momentum in game situations. Play has to stay at a fast pace because of time constraints. Players have to know their positions and rotations and move quickly from one play to the next. Players must focus on keeping control of the serve and scoring points. A side must constantly come from behind and then finish the game quickly before the score switches.

Directions:

1. Set up two teams of six each in a scrimmage situation, with both sides engaging in regular match play.

2. The coach or manager keeps score.

3. Every 60 seconds, the score switches until one side scores the winning point.

4. Play to a designated point total or time limit.

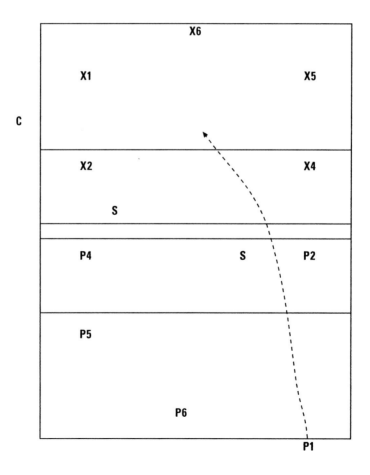

DRILL #85: S.O.S. (SIDE-OUT SCORING)

Number of Players: 12

Number of Balls: 1 or more

Objective: To practice a game-like situation where scoring only occurs with a sideout offense—in other words, only the first play off the serve earns a point. The drill truly enhances the necessity of both, incorporating a strong sideout offense and intense serving into one's program. The games may take longer than normal; however, the focus of the players is intense throughout the drill.

Directions:

1. Set up two teams (A and B) of six players in regularly assigned playing positions.

2. Team A begins the drill by serving to Team B. If the serving team digs and returns the ball, the rally simply continues through completion.

3. The serve then goes to the team winning the rally; however, no points will be awarded. Teams may only score points by effectively using the side-out offense or serving an ace, which should always be rewarded.

4. A serving error will result in a side out, thus a point is awarded to the receivers.

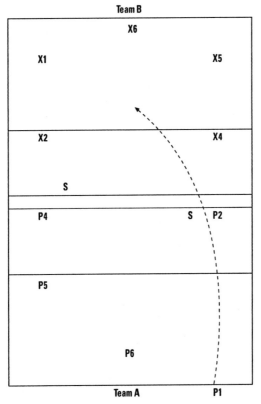

DRILL #86: SIX-ON-SIX QUICK-MIDDLE-DEEP HIT

Number of Players: 12

Number of Balls: 12 or more

Objective: To emphasize team defensive skills, transition to middle attack, back-court hitting and coverage underneath the block.

Directions:

1. Players begin in switched defensive positions with the setters in the front row. All outside sets are to back-row players. All middle sets are quick (the dump is okay).

2. Play it as a wash drill to six, giving each team a free ball from the opposite baseline.

3. Incorporate no rotation. The coach can move personnel when a team has scored three points (switch front and back row).

4. The slowness of the free balls will keep the pace moderate. Be sure to put a new ball into play immediately after a ball hits the floor. This is a drill the coach can stop briefly for instruction without killing its momentum.

Scoring:

1. Play to six wash points. Do not hesitate to play a second game if the first one goes too quickly. The winner does not have to win by two.

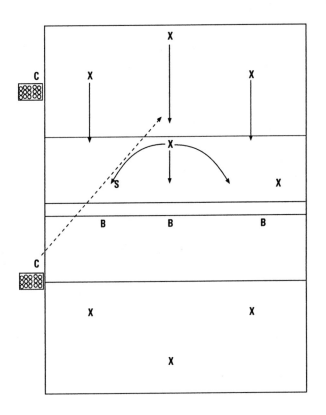

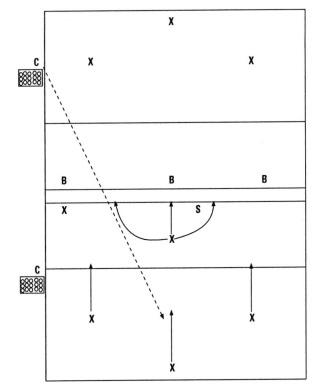

DRILL #87: THREE-POINT DRILL

Number of Players: 10 or more

Number of Balls: Steady supply

Objective: To simulate game-like transition for down ball and free ball situations. It also encourages proper positioning, footwork and defensive technique.

Directions:

1. On Court B, Team B serves/defends.

2. On Court A, Team A is in serve receive formation.

3. Team B serves the ball, and it is played out to termination.

4. At termination of initial serve, Team A goes to defensive mode, and one coach (C1) then hits a topspin or a free ball to Team A, which must play with Team B to termination.

5. At termination of C1's ball, C2 then hits a topspin or free ball to Team A, which plays to termination.

6. Team A gets three chances to make three points before it is allowed to rotate to the next position.

7. If Team A does not get three points off the three attempts, then repeat the process until successful.

Scoring:

1. Team A: One point for termination of play on high or regular attacks; two points for termination on quick attacks; zero points for losing rally in any manner. This goes until all rotations have been completed, then substitute and begin again.

Variations:

1. Create point totals to emphasize various attacks, including offspeed, down line, cross-court, tool, etc.

2. Have Team B rotate to a new server on each Team A rotation or anytime to get new serve types.

3. If Team A fails on initial attack, then ensure the opportunity to run the two-point play from a C1 or C2 ball.

4. Earn more points for certain rotations to make it more difficult.

5. Start Team A in any rotation to begin the drill.

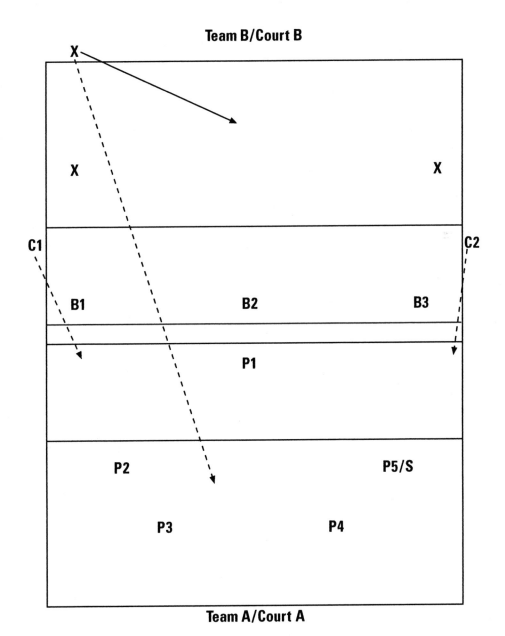

Team B/Court B

Team A/Court A

DRILL #88: THREE-TEAM WASH

Number of Players: 18 or more (teams of six)

Number of Balls: Steady supply

Objective: This drill accommodates large squads with an active and intense multi-skill activity. It allows the coaching staff the flexibility to develop first-, second- and third-string players within the same activity.

Directions:

1. The drill begins with one team on the "winner's side" and another on the "challenge side," which is similar to many king/queen of the court drills. The third team waits to get on the court behind the baseline and out of the playing area on the challenge side.

2. The serve is initiated by the challengers, and the rally is played out, followed by a "wash rally" (free ball) entered on the challenge side. Normal wash variations of little points and big points may be used, but when the designated number of big points is achieved, a few things can occur. The serving team must win both rallies to advance to the winner's side.

3. The team that loses is off the court. If the team on the winner's side wins again, it gets to rotate and face the next challenger. However, if the team on the challenge side wins, it merely "advances" to the winner's side and stays in the same rotation. In other words, a rotation can only occur with a victory (designated big points) from the winner's side.

Variations:

1. Team A may be required to achieve three big points to rotate and Teams B and C only two. In the case where two groups are slightly better than the third, the drill will provide several opportunities for the third group, but most washes will occur between the two evenly matched teams, thus enhancing their experience as well.

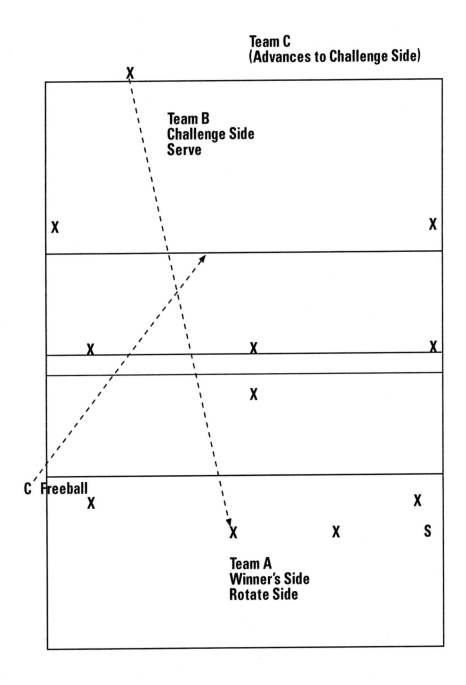

Team C
(Advances to Challenge Side)

Team B
Challenge Side
Serve

C Freeball

Team A
Winner's Side
Rotate Side

DRILL #89: VORTEX

Number of Players: 12

Number of Balls: 12 to 15

Objective: To help players develop proper team play and transition.

Directions:

1. Divide the players into two teams.

2. Team A serves to Team B. The teams play the ball out; the coach (C) tosses another ball to the team that wins that rally after the ball is dead.

3. The second ball is played out until one team puts the ball away. Immediately, C sends another ball into the winner's court.

Scoring:

1. When a team creates a positive (kill, stuff block, etc.), a point is earned. The score is a running cumulative score within that sequence. If Team A serves to Team B, then Team B passes, sets and spikes; the result is a kill, and the score is 1-0 in favor of Team B. This sequence continues until one of the teams achieves the target goal.

2. Once the game is over, the winning team rotates one position, and the team that received the last time will now serve. Only the winning team rotates. The team that rotates through all six rotations is the winner.

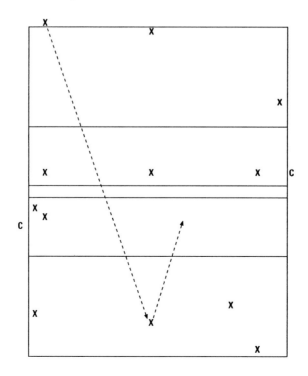

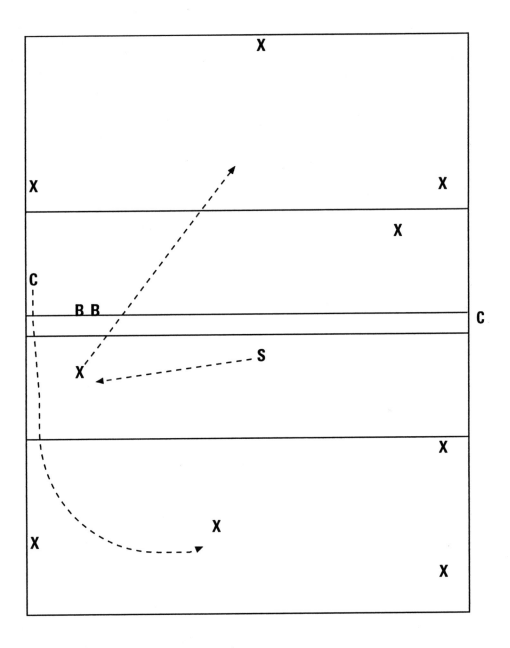

CHAPTER 9

DEFENSE DRILLS

Drill #90: Acceleration

Number of Players: 9

Number of Balls: Steady supply

Objective: This drill is excellent for teams that play a basic perimeter defense. Run-throughs and emergency skills will receive emphasis.

Directions:

1. The coach (C) stands on one side of the court with a cart of volleyballs and several feeders (X).

2. One right back player (RB), one middle back player (MB), and one left back player (LB) stand on the end line of the other side of the court with one "on deck" (X) player in each spot as well.

3. C tips the ball to force RB to accelerate and dig the ball to target (T). The ball is then tipped to the MB and the LB. Once a player digs the ball, he/she immediately retreats to the end line in preparation for the next ball.

4. C goes through this procedure from a left-side attack, middle attack and right-side attack. The key points for the players are to stay low, accelerate to and through the ball and to go for every ball.

Variations:

1. Players can go through the drill for a predetermined number of attempts.

2. Players can go through the drill for a predetermined number of perfect passes.

3. Players can go through the drill for a predetermined time.

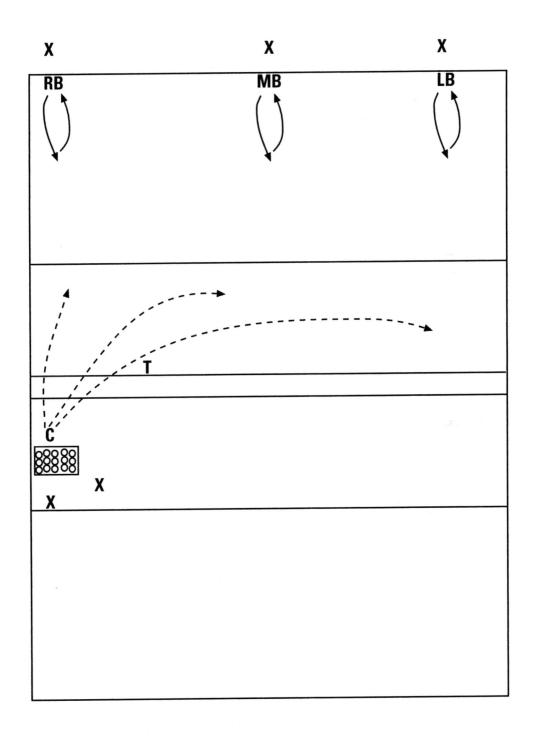

DRILL #91: COACH-ON-THREE

Number of Players: 3

Number of Balls: Steady supply

Objective: This drill is coach-controlled in terms of difficulty and intensity, and it provides for a large number of ball contacts. It requires good court communication by players and allows them to get a lot of digging reps.

Directions:

1. Two coaches (C1, C2) position themselves on top of stable platforms and hit at three players (X) in back-row defensive positions.

2. C2 hits three balls from the left front position; then C1 hits three balls from the right front position.

3. The players must achieve 15 controlled digs into the target area (T), along with 15 hittable sets, to finish the drill.

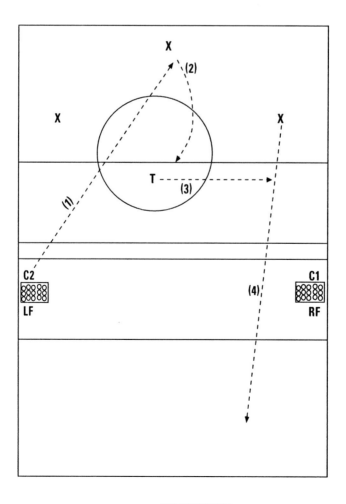

DRILL #92: FOUR-PERSON WITH A SETTER

Number of Players: 12

Number of Balls: Steady supply

Objective: This drill assists in developing team defense and the ability to play next to teammates.

Directions:

1. One player occupies each of the following positions: right back (RB), middle back (MB), left back (LB), left front (LF) and right front (S).

2. One coach (C2) stands in the right front, simulating a left-side attack, while another coach (C1) stands in the left front, simulating a right-side attack.

3. C2 initiates play by attacking a ball to any of the diggers. S then sets the dug ball to either C1 or C2, and live play continues.

4. When a ball hits the floor, another ball is immediately put into play.

5. All five players must stay alive as diggers—emphasize "on-help" defense. The diggers practice reading the hitter and communicating with teammates.

Variations:

1. C controls the difficulty of the drill.

2. Players can be rotated either according to time (three minutes per group) or after a mistake is made.

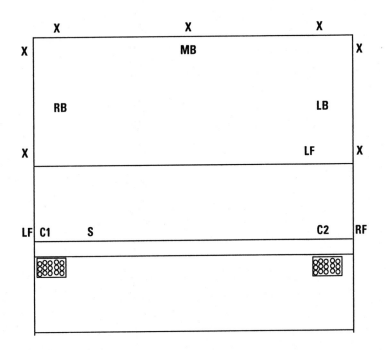

DRILL #93: DEFENSIVE MOVEMENT

Number of Players: 6–8

Number of Balls: Steady supply

Objective: To teach court movement from one defensive position to another, including digging hard hits, tips, and free balls. The drill also helps develop foot speed, quickness to the ball and conditioning.

Directions:

1. Divide the team into groups of three or four players (X) to start at the attack line, ready to backpedal along the sideline.

2. One coach (C1) slaps the ball to begin backpedal action.

3. Each player (P) will receive five balls: a spike and a tip from C1, a free ball from C2 and a spike and a tip from C3.

4. Each player in that group will repeat each sequence three to five times or for two to three minutes.

5. As soon as a player digs the second ball, C2 must toss the free ball when the player is ready, and the second player should be ready to backpedal. Switch teams either at the end of the sequence or when time is up.

Variations:

1. Players with good control can take the place of C1, 2 or 3.

2. Coaches can stand on the other side of the net on a stable platform.

3. The drill can be modified for beginners by receiving only three balls: a spike, a tip and a free ball.

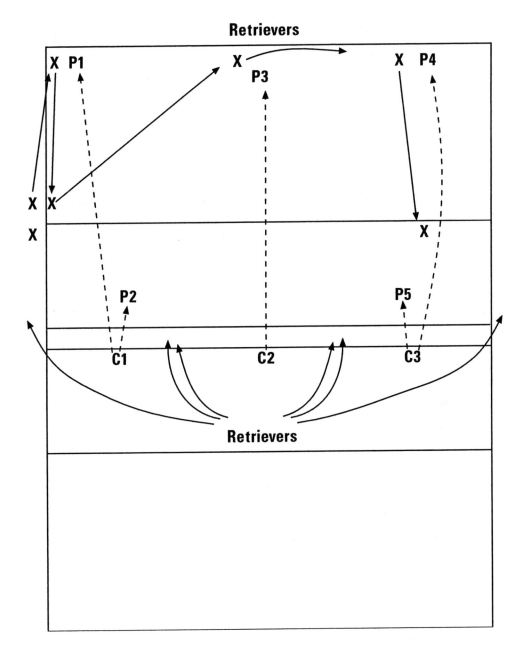

DRILL #94: KAMIKAZE

Number of Players: 3

Number of Balls: Steady supply

Objective: This is a good reaction drill that tests players for quickness and timing in terms of defense.

Directions:

1. Three players (P1, P2, P3) set up on one side of the net behind the attack line.

2. The coach (C) stands on a stable platform and hits/tosses all types of balls at the players in rapid succession.

3. Non-participating players retrieve the balls and feed them immediately to C.

4. C sets the time limit.

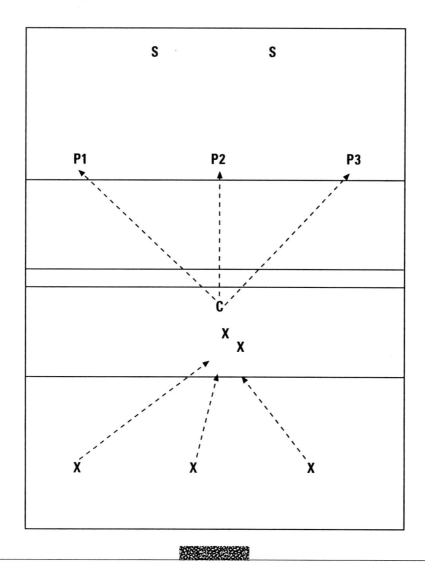

DRILL #95: MOVING TEAM DEFENSE

Number of Players: 3

Number of Balls: Steady supply

Objective: This drill forces the players to stop when a hitter is making contact with the ball (even when they are out of position). It forces players to communicate more and louder (i.e., players must communicate each time they switch positions). Players must keep their platforms extended in front of them at all times, and they must travel low.

Directions:

1. Split the team into groups of threes. One group starts in "starting D," as shown in the diagram (X1, X2, X3).

2. The coach (C) is standing on the same side of the net. C tosses the ball anywhere on the court (tip or off-speed shot).

3. The players have one or two contacts to play the ball back to C and then rotate clockwise.

4. The players rotate each time they play the ball back to C.

5. Run the drill for a set amount of time before a new group comes in. The clock is reset each time the players do not communicate or go for a ball or stop at the point of contact. (The coach is only tipping, passing, or hitting off-speed shots or setting anywhere on the court, but not directly at the players. Make the players move and learn to recover quickly, since they have to rotate.)

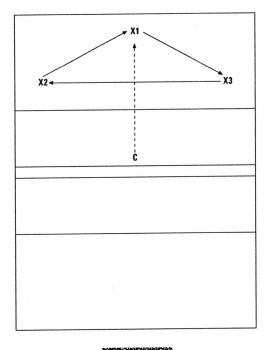

DRILL #96: RODEO

Number of Players: 6 or more

Number of Balls: Steady supply

Objective: This drill works on having the athlete move quickly to dig the ball, focusing on blocking the ball and then sprinting to run down the ball hit over his/her head. It keeps the players moving with many repetitions.

Directions:

1. Players set up in a group of three or four (X) and start off the court on the right side. The coach (C) starts the drill with a "slap" of the ball.

2. The first player moves onto the court (1) to dig the first attack.

3. The same player then sprints to the left side of the court (2) to dig the right side.

4. The player then sprints to the net (3) to block a ball and finishes with a sprint to the deep court (4) to run down the ball, which is thrown over his/her head.

5. All balls should be passed to the target (T). All off-court players are retrieving balls and feeding C.

6. Dig 30 balls to T to finish the drill. Rotate the next group in and continue. The drill can also be done from either a left- or right-side attack.

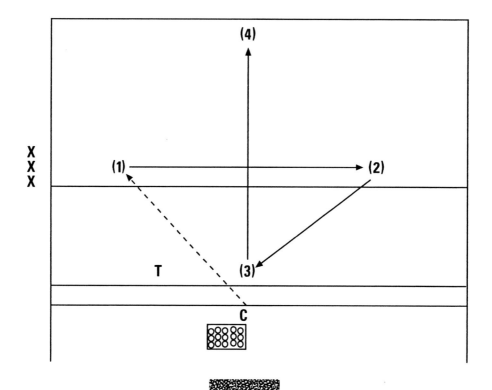

DRILL #97: TEAM DEFENSE VS. COACH

Number of Players: 6

Number of Balls: Steady supply

Objective: This is a controlled drill that allows for excellent teaching of exact defense situations. Proper positioning is required on each play and gives the coach the opportunity to repeat exact situations.

Directions:

1. The coach (C) attacks balls against a team of players.

2. The players must play good defense and convert the transition to attack successfully.

3. Players should be rotated frequently. Play continues for a predetermined amount of time or a certain number of successful attacks.

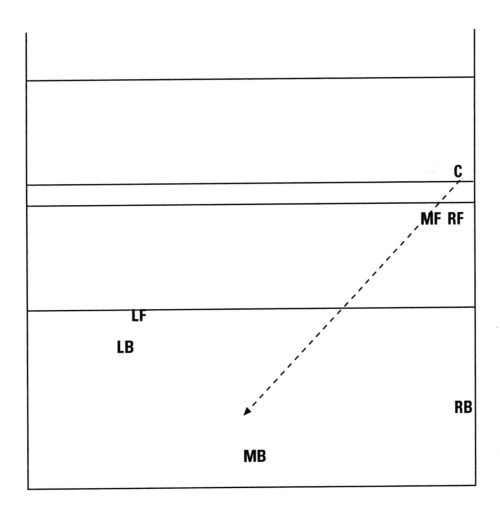

DRILL #98: THREE BLIND MICE

Number of Players: 10

Number of Balls: Steady supply

Objective: This drill is designed to encourage teamwork and quick thinking on the court. Through this drill, players develop an ability to attack the ball from anywhere on the court, but from behind the 3-meter line.

Directions:

1. Three players (P) lie on their stomachs about 5 to 10 feet into the court, facing the end line. (Do not let them look back—they must react on sound only.)

2. The coach (C) is positioned across the net, just beyond the attack line, and anywhere along it. Toss or hit the ball over—mix it up, if possible.

3. The players (P) spring up as C bounces the ball on the floor or calls, "Ball," as it is tossed across the net to alert the diggers. P passes to the setter (S), who then sets any of the three attackers/passers who must attack the ball. Only these types of attacks count, and players may attack from anywhere on the court, but from behind the 3-meter line.

4. Players return to the end lines to wait until the next round. Make sure the players get in a different line each time.

Variations:

1. Do not have a designated setter at the target position. Have the passers become the setter.

2. Keep time and see how many total attacks for the drill are completed in the designated number of minutes.

3. Set an attack number goal for each group or individual.

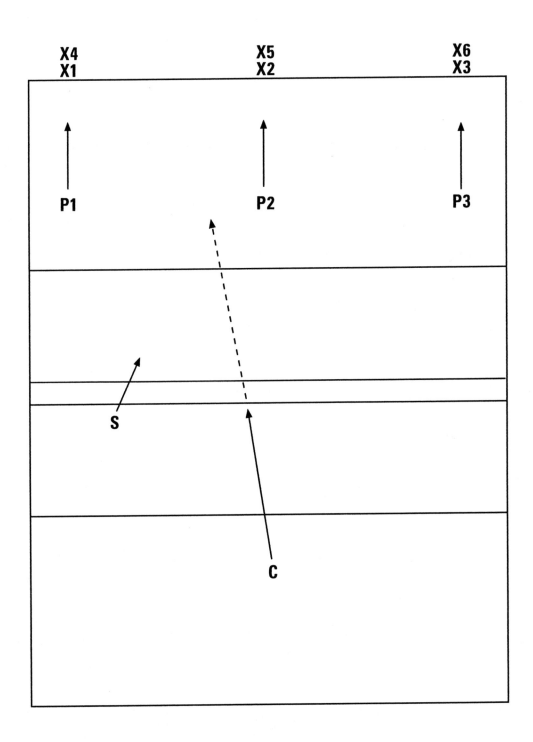

DRILL #99: THREE-POSITION DRILL

Number of Players: 6 or more

Number of Balls: Steady supply

Objective: This drill is used to provide opportunities to dig a deep spike, a tip and an off-court deflection.

Directions:

1. The coach (C) attacks the ball to the digger (X), who digs it to the target (T).

2. X hustles to pick up a very short tip and plays it to T.

3. Immediately, X hustles to run down the high ball that C tosses outside the court area.

4. C then immediately begins again by attacking the ball to the same position with another player.

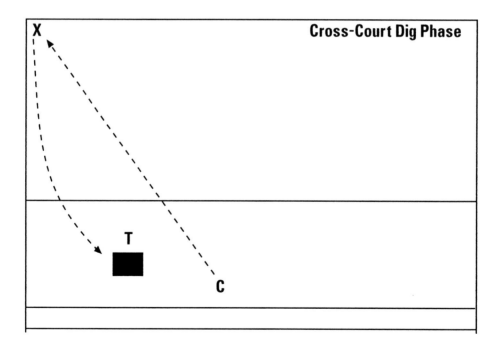

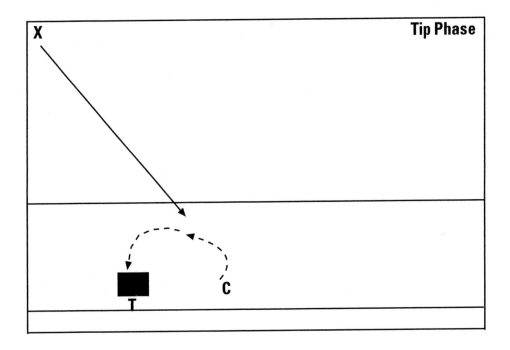

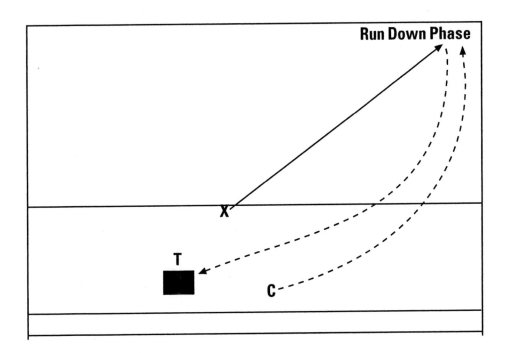

DRILL #100: TROUBLE PLAYS

Number of Players: 5 or more

Number of Balls: 3 or more

Objective: This drill entices players to play a ball out of the net on two contacts, stressing communication and the ability to work together.

Directions:

1. The coach (C) simulates a bad dig by hitting the ball into the net or off the court.

2. Players should stay low and play the ball out of the net. The players have two contacts to get the ball into the opponent's court.

3. After each play, the players rotate—right front becomes a retriever, and the retriever hands a ball to C and gets into the court in middle back position.

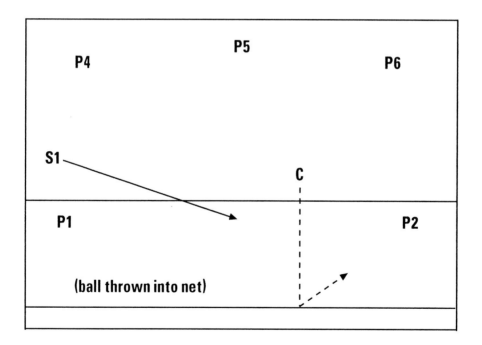

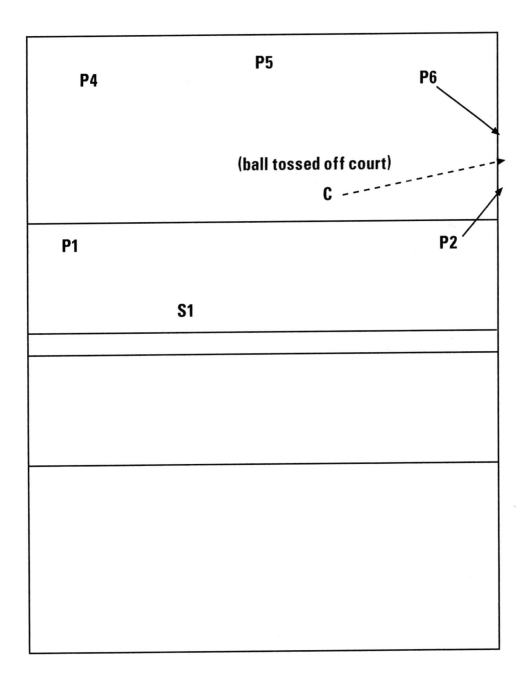

DRILL #101: UP-AND-BACK DIGGING

Number of Players: 6–12

Number of Balls: Steady supply

Objective: This drill encourages forward and backward defensive movement training. It is very challenging and teaches reading, covering and court balancing.

Directions:

1. Set up three players (X) on defense who are to cover and balance the court entirely.

2. The coach (C) begins by tossing a short or deep ball over the net. The players must play the ball to the target (T), then immediately move back to dig a toss to the hitters (H).

3. To score a point, the defenders must get both balls up to T. If they do not touch a ball, the tally goes back to zero. The defensive team must score 10 points to get out of the drill.

4. Do this from all three hitting positions.

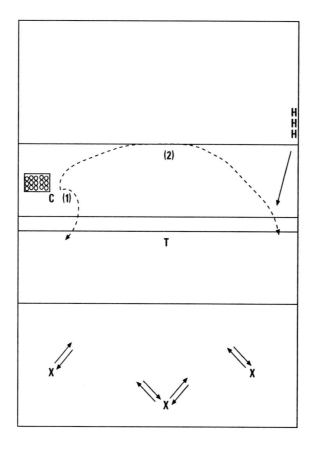

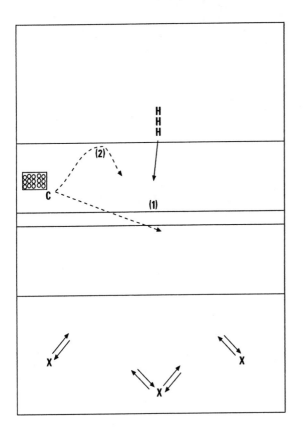

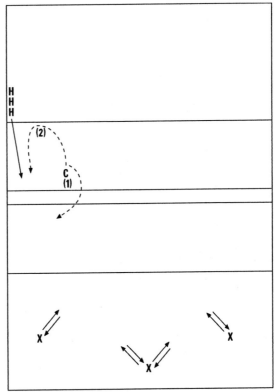

Attack Power: Velocity of attack; overall team strength.

Commit Block: One player (usually the middle blocker) jumps with the quick attacker.

Cut: Imparting a sharp direction to a spike; to hit against the body line (e.g., for a right-handed player hitting power from left front, the cut shot is to hit back toward the sideline, on the same sideline as the hitter).

D-Set: Antiquated term that means to set behind the setter.

Dump: A ball that has been attacked or sent over the net by the setter on the second contact.

51: The first tempo attack (1 foot high) from area 5 of net (directly in front of setter).

52: The second tempo attack (2 feet high) from area 5 of net (directly in front of setter).

First Tempo Set: Quick set (1); e.g., 51, 71, 91.

Hit Line: A straight, sideline attack.

"J" Stroke: A "recovery skill" forearm pass technique in which the thumbs are turned up, with the elbows bent (forming a "J").

On-Help defense: A player's defensive floor position/body posture which allows him/her to play the ball in front of the body and toward other teammates.

Overpass: A ball that is passed across the net.

Perimeter Defense: A backcourt defense in which four players arrange themselves near the boundaries (end lines/sidelines of the court).

Pipe: Set to a back-row attacker in the middle of the court.

Play Set: A set of medium height (usually near the middle of the court) that constitutes a play in combination with a quick set.

Rally-Score: A point is awarded each time a rally ends.

Recovery Skill: Regaining body posture and position after executing emergency skills; the act of recovering the ball on the outside of the court or playing a tip.

Run-Through: Playing a ball in a low body posture while moving through the point of contact.

Slide: A particular attack approach that includes a last-minute move along the net.

Stuff Block: To block the ball to the floor.

31: A low, quick set from area 3 of net; commonly referred to as a "shoot" set.

3-Option pass: An ideal pass that allows the setter to choose any setting option.

Tip: The one-handed placement of the ball with the fingers.

Transition: The shift from defense to offense.

Wash Scoring: In a "wash" drill, "big" points and "little" points are given (e.g., the receiving team must convert a serve reception to receive a "little" point, then convert a free ball for a second "little" point in order to receive one "big" point).

Wave Rotation: Method of rotating players during drills (e.g., the entire front row on Side A rotates to the front row on Side B; the entire back row on Side A rotates to the front row on Side A, with the front row on Side B moving to the back row of Side B).

CONTRIBUTORS

(*institution where contributor was coaching at the time the drill first appeared in *Power Tips*; current whereabouts unknown)

Emilio Agrait (Borinquen Gardens Volleyball Club, Puerto Rico)

*Karyn Altman (Massachusetts Institute of Technology, Cambridge, Mass.)

*Ernie Arill (Miami Sunset High School, Miami, Fla.)

Arnie Ball (Indiana/Purdue–Fort Wayne, Fort Wayne, Ind.)

Andy Banachowski (UCLA, Los Angeles, Calif.)

Zoe Bell (Providence High School, Charlotte, N.C.)

*Eileen Beninga (Waterloo West High School, Waterloo, Iowa)

Peter N. Bilous (Bishop Kearney High School, Rochester, N.Y.)

Larry Bock (Juniata College, Huntingdon, Pa.)

Peggy Bradley-Doppes (University of Michigan, Ann Arbor, Mich.; current SWA)

Stephen Burkard (Lafayette High School, Lafayette, Mo.)

Curt Burns (Avon High School, Avon, Conn.)

Nick Cheronis (University of Florida, Gainesville, Fla.)

*Maribel Colon (Antilles High School, San Juan, Puerto Rico)

*Mark Colvin (Wabash Valley College, Mt. Carmel, Ill.)

*Dean Conk (The Master's College, Santa Clarita, Calif.)

*Brent Curtice (Hotchkiss High School, Hotchkiss, Colo.)

Tere Dail (University of North Carolina–Greensboro, Greensboro, N.C.)

Steve Dallman (University of Missouri–Kansas City, Kansas City, Mo.)

*Lynn Davidson (Ohio University, Athens, Ohio)

Joel Dearing (Springfield College, Springfield, Mass.)

Susie Fleenor (Norfolk Academy, Norfolk, Va.)

Bob Gambardella (USA Volleyball, Colorado Springs, Colo.)

Dave Gantt (Montana State University, Bozeman, Mont.)

Ed Garrett (Colorado Christian University, Lakewood, Colo.)

Zen Golembiowsky, Educational Sports Products

Sue Gozansky (University of California–Riverside, Riverside, Calif.)

Judy Green (University of Alabama, Tuscaloosa, Ala.)

Jerry Gregg (Cypress High School, Cypress, Calif.)

*Bonnie Hamryka (Tiffin University, Tiffin, Ohio)

*R. Doug Harbottle (Cal Juniors Volleyball Club, Anaheim, Calif.)

Naomi Hatfield (Black Hills State University, Spearfish, S.D.)

Mark Herrin (University of Central Oklahoma, Edmond, Okla.)

*Lori Hughes (Emerson College, Boston, Mass.)

Paul Jacoby (Ohio Valley College, Parkersburg, W.V.)

*Cristine Jarrett (Chatham Central High School, Chatham, N.Y.)

Tom Justice (Lock Haven University, Lock Haven, Pa.)

Mary Kaminski (Northeastern University, Boston, Mass.)

Ulana Keer (BuxMont High School, Sellersville, Pa.)

Pat Kendrick (George Mason University, Fairfax, Va.)

Bonnie Kenny (University of Massachusetts, Springfield, Mass.)

John Kessel (USA Volleyball, Colorado Springs, Colo.)

Judy Kirkpatrick (Athletes in Action, Lebanon, Ohio)

Janice Kruger (University of Maryland, College Park, Md.)

Steve Larkin (Eckerd College, St. Petersburg, Fla.)

Frank Lavrisha (Regis University, Denver, Colo.)

Lisa Love (University of Southern California, Los Angeles, Calif.; current associate athletics director)

Scott Luster (Bradley University, Peoria, Ill.)

*Sean Madden (Gonzaga University, Spokane, Wash.)

Nabil M. Mardini (Pierce College, Woodland Hills, Calif.)

*Marilyn Mather (U.S. Coast Guard Academy, New London, Conn.)

Tod Mattox (The Bishop's School, San Diego, Calif.)

Bob McCarthy (Central Union High School, Fresno, Calif.)

Duncan McFarland (University of California–San Diego, San Diego, Calif.)

*Jerrie McGahan (University of Denver, Denver, Colo.)

Jacquie Medina

*Karen Mendes (Bryant College, Smithfield, R.I.)

Douglas B. Milner (Boerne High School, Boerne, Texas)

*Julie Moffit (Upper Iowa University, Fayette, Iowa)

Kristi Nelson-Hitz (Lincoln High School, Lincoln, Neb.)

Sandy Novak (Sahuaro High School, Tucson, Ariz.)

*Pat Olson (Union High School, Biggsville, Ill.)

Mark Pavlik (Penn State University, University Park, Pa.)

*Bill Peer (U.S. Air Force Academy, Colorado Springs, Colo.)

Jane Peterson (Central Lakes College, Brainerd, Minn.)

Suzie Pignetti (Butler High School, Matthews, N.C.)

Geri Polvino (Eastern Kentucky University, Richmond, Ky.)

Ken Preston (University of California–Santa Barbara, Santa Barbara, Calif.)

*Michael J. Puritz (University of California–Irvine, Irvine, Calif.)

Tom Read (Saddleback Valley Unified School District, Fresno, Calif.)

Colleen Richert (Bakersfield College, Bakersfield, Calif.)

Mark Ridley (Muskegon Orchard View High School, Muskegon, Mich.)

*Terri Robbie (Central Michigan University, Mt. Pleasant, Mich.)

Russ Rose (Penn State University, University Park, Pa.)

*Marc Rose-Gold (Crescent Valley High School, Corvallis, Ore.)

Judy Sackfield (University of Alabama–Birmingham, Birmingham, Ala.)

Richard Scott (University of Montana, Missoula, Mont.)

*Stu Serine (Manteo High School, Manteo, N.C.)

Don Shaw (Stanford University, Stanford, Calif.)

*Ron Shayka (George Mason University, Fairfax, Va.)

Stuart Sherman (Graceland College, Lamoni, Iowa)

Tom Shoji (University of Southern Colorado, Pueblo, Colo.)

Rick Squiers (University of Nebraska–Kearney, Kearney, Neb.)

*Rudy Suwara (San Diego State University, San Diego, Calif.)

Doug Van Oort (Kirkwood Community College, Cedar Rapids, Iowa)

Barbara Viera (University of Delaware, Newark, Del.)

*Stuart Wahl (Fox Lane High School, Bedford, N.Y.)

Rosie Wegrich (Cal Poly Pomona, Pomona, Calif.)

Mike Welch (University of North Florida, Jacksonville, Fla.)

*Marjorie Whinery (Modesto Junior College, Modesto, Calif.)

*Christa White (Apple Valley High School, Apple Valley, Calif.)

Hank Wysocki (Siena College, Albany, N.Y.)